BUILD IT RIGHT

Wisdom for Business Owners
& Those Who Want to Be

BUILD IT RIGHT

Wisdom for Business Owners
& Those Who Want to Be

JOHN C. BENNETT

XULON PRESS

Xulon Press
2301 Lucien Way #415
Maitland, FL 32751
407.339.4217
www.xulonpress.com

Paperback ISBN-13: 978-1-6628-2223-0
Ebook ISBN-13: 978-1-6628-2224-7

TABLE OF CONTENTS:

DEDICATION:

I dedicate this book to my Savior and Lord, Jesus Christ. He has given me the knowledge and wisdom to build my career and the courage to share this wisdom with others. When all is said and done and my time on this earth is through, it is my relationship with Him that is most important. Success in this life is temporal, but a relationship with God through Jesus Christ is eternal. Matthew 6:33.

BUILD IT RIGHT

**Wisdom for Business Owners
& Those Who Want to Be**

INTRODUCTION:

*B*uild It Right is a book for business owners in every stage of their business. Those who are currently working for someone else and dreaming of starting their own business, those who are in the initial years of running their own business, and those who have owned their own business for 30 years or more all can benefit from the wisdom contained herein. A well-built and well-run business is established on principles that are consistent, no matter what stage of the business cycle one is in.

Join me on this journey and absorb the wisdom I've learned from my 25-year career in banking that has been spent helping business owners to achieve maximum profitability and balanced growth in the businesses that they have chosen to start. You'll learn about many of the things these business owners did that made them super successful, while also learning about mistakes they made. This will help you avoid some of these pitfalls in your current or future business.

From a banker's perspective, this book will share advice on how you, a business owner, can be "laughing all the way to the bank." These timeless principles come from my working with hundreds of successful businesses. Build It Right will give you tools that can help you to build a strong and highly profitable business.

This book will share wisdom that can assist you with achieving financial wealth and independence. However, the hope is not simply that you get wealthy through your business, but that you also achieve a high quality of life that gives you an overall well-rounded form of success. In the long run, this will mean more to you than just becoming wealthy in financial terms.

The goal of this book is to help business owners to build their business in such a way as to best ensure a thriving, long-term entity that will benefit them, their employees, and society in general. My passion is guiding business owners of all kinds to get the most out of their company; it is a ministry that God has given me. While I have no desire to start my own business, I admire those who do and I love sitting on "this side of the desk," helping those business owners to thrive.

I wrote this book because it is my hope that my knowledge and expertise, coupled with my dedication to helping people, will make a difference to those who are bold enough to build and run their own business. That business could be in software development, engineering, practicing medicine, feeding others in a restaurant, music publishing, or a million other varieties. A well-run business is a well-run business, no matter the industry.

Coming from a banker's perspective, it might surprise you to see that this book is less about detailed financial concepts and analysis, and more about overall wisdom and philosophy. The reason this book is formatted in this way is simple. These overall concepts, philosophies, and pieces of wisdom, when implemented, can lead to the financial success of the business, and the owners as well.

Financials don't drive the business; the business drives the financials. All of the financial analysis and reporting are merely a snapshot or score card of how well or how poorly a business owner has made choices each day in regard to their preparation, execution, business plan, employees, and customers. So, to focus too much strictly on financial concepts and analysis at this point would be like putting the "cart before the horse." If the horse is leading properly with appropriate strength, the cart will follow. It is the same way with financial success following wise business formation and leadership. Of course, this does not negate the proper management of your business from the cues given in your monthly and quarterly financial analysis; it simply puts this analysis in proper perspective.

The wisdom in this book comes from over 25 years of working with business clients. This experience has afforded me the unique privilege of having a "bird's-eye view" of all of the financials and a "behind the scenes" look at the decisions that were made from day to day by business owners. If you follow the wisdom outlined in this book, it can make a positive difference in the financial reports you receive on your business each quarter and each year.

Of course, no one can guarantee your success as a business owner. However, there are time-tested principles that, when applied correctly, will give you the best possible chance of building and maintaining a thriving business that is financially successful. In the same manner, ignoring or refuting these time-tested principles has caused many business owners to end up with a failed business and in personal financial ruin.

Whether you have run a successful business for 40 years or are simply contemplating starting your own company, I believe you will find useful information and encouragement in the pages that follow. It will give you a different perspective on your business.

This book is honest and forthright enough to tell you some things that others might not point out, who wish to profit from your business or who make it a priority to stay in your good graces. The goal is to give you solid information that will truly benefit you for a lifetime and for the lifetime of your business.

If you're ready to take a concentrated look at yourself and your business to see if any changes need to be made to shore up your weaknesses and lead with your strengths, then let's get it on. If this book helps you to implement even one idea that makes your business more sound or successful, then its purpose will have been served.

—All My Best, John C. Bennett

CHAPTER 1:

FOR THE LOVE OF IT

Having spent the past quarter of a century with a bird's eye view of hundreds, maybe thousands, of company financials, I began to notice certain characteristics that were evident in most of the successful ones. I also noticed some potholes that many of the unsuccessful businesses stepped into, derailing their companies. Out of all the various industries, different business sizes, and distinct personalities of the business owners, certain common denominators were present in the successes. This realization is what prompted me, a banker who works with all types of businesses, to share my insights on what makes a business successful.

For 25 years, I've questioned and advised the decisions, expertise, and processes of business owners who came to me for a loan to further grow their business. Therefore, I felt that it was time for me to be the one to spill the beans (since I am a bean counter) concerning what I've been privileged to see through many years, and through a few thousand corporate tax returns, financial statements, and business plans.

Let's start with the beginning. How did the successful business owners with whom I've worked become good enough at something to make a business out of it, and actually convince people to spend their hard-earned money to pay them for doing something they enjoy anyway? Did you notice that I used the word "enjoy"? The first characteristic of successful business owners is that they have found something they enjoy. It is something they enjoy doing enough to spend countless hours, days, and years becoming proficient at it so that one day people gladly will pay them for their expertise, or in the case of a product, for the rendering created from their expertise.

Of all those successful business owners, not one of them went into an area that they didn't have a strong interest or passion for being in. Therefore, most really don't consider it "work" because the field they're in is so exciting and fun for them. However, the financial reporting, the people management, the tough decisions—that's work. But considering the field they're in, it's a comfortable fit for them and there is at least some level of joy and play associated with it in the business owner's mind.

On a national scale, do you think Steven Jobs liked playing with technology and inventing? Do you think Mark Zuckerberg has a passion for technology and connecting people? Do you think Warren Buffett enjoys learning about businesses and investing in them? The joy and the passion must be there. Otherwise, it's just a job and one never will be able to stick with it long enough to become truly successful at it.

People who are the best at their jobs, careers, and businesses have an uncanny ability to see the service they provide as an extension of who they are. They don't mind if you ask their professional advice at church or at a restaurant because their business is just what they do to serve others. It is their little niche in life, their area of service to humanity. And besides, they're "darn good at it" and they like to educate others on a subject on which they happen to be an expert. They tend to see their business as more of a "calling" than simply a career or a way to make a living.

Of all the ingredients that must be in place to be successful, the passion of the business owner is the most important. I always tell people to remember the two "Ps"—Passion and Persistence, and without the Passion, there is no Persistence.

Let's break it down to a ground level. Throughout this book I will talk about a few longtime clients in general terms to protect their privacy and my professional and fiduciary responsibilities. Client Number One always had a love for cars. He went toward this passion in his career and, over time, he saw a need to provide personalized long-term parking services for cars owned by business travelers while they traveled by air out of town. Because he followed his passion and treated his clients likes kings and queens, he grew his business into a very successful enterprise that was profitable for many years. He later sold the business to a competitor and was able to have a fine retirement. That's the power of passion and the payoff for loving what you do.

If you are considering starting your own business, be sure to focus on the right field and the right industry that combines your talents, experience, and passion or excitement. In the life of any business owner, there will be many late nights, along with many challenges. Without having a basic underlying passion for what you do, it will prove difficult to forge through these common obstacles that always come along with any business.

Perhaps you are already running a business and you lack the passion, joy, and love for it. Consider redirecting a portion of your business to encompass areas that tap into your passions and what you love to do or be around. You even may find that you have put down roots in the wrong industry, and can work toward selling your current business and investing the proceeds into something that better fits you. If this is too drastic of a move for you at this time, you still can find small ways to gravitate some of your business talents toward areas that give you more excitement and fulfillment. For instance, if you own a catering company, but have always had a strong passion for being involved in music, why not target catering some music events and festivals? That way you can apply your business expertise and skill set along with an atmosphere that you are sure to enjoy.

My father used to tell me that "the money won't get you up on Monday morning." That means you must have more than simply a solid paycheck if you desire to wake up each week with a fresh quest for adventure in your chosen career and profession. To me, one of the true tragedies in life is someone who has spent their whole working career doing something that they never really enjoyed. Since we spend more time at work than with anything else, we should insist on our work life being a combination of our greatest talents, passions, and experience.

Don't settle for simply making a living, especially if you are the one building a business. Be sure you take the time on the front end to engage in an area of business that will keep you excited for the long haul. As some people have said, "If you love what you do for a living, you'll never have to work a day in your life." Life is short, so insist upon doing something you love. If others see your love and passion for your business, your job of selling your products or services will become much easier, and others will catch your passion as well.

Passion creates and sustains energy. This is the fuel that will enable you to make it through any challenges you may face as a business owner. Be sure you do whatever is necessary to find your area of passion prior to investing your life savings into starting a business. Get feedback from those who know and love you best. Take advantage of various special-interest tests that can lead you to your passion. Study the times and experiences in your life that have yielded you the most joy.

You also may find out that it is not only a particular field of industry that gives you added passion, but it also may be the type of work you do. For instance, someone who likes to perform in front of people may get as much satisfaction from being the owner and CEO of a logistics company that enables her to be in front of people on a regular basis, and to speak publicly, as she would as a professional opera singer or Broadway actor.

Someone who loves to interact with people, network, and build relationships may find as much satisfaction in being a salesperson for a business as they would in being a politician or a pastor. Also, a person who loves helping people and investing in their lives may get as much fulfillment in running a business that provides a necessary service or builds and markets a life-changing product as they would in being a social worker or a healthcare provider.

Everything that is worthwhile in this life needs to be done or produced. When you find what you love, you can tailor how you produce this product or service in such a way as to utilize your strengths, passions, and talents, in conjunction with excellence, to find both success and fulfillment. Therefore, you need to dig deep when looking for that right combination of job responsibilities, industry specifics, and fields of interest that will allow you to operate at your best and highest use. One thing's for sure: Once you find it, you will know.

For example, what if you have a deep love for playing music and a strong desire to perform in front of people? However, instead of a professional level of music talent, you have tremendous financial skills, relationship building strengths, or highly developed organizational skills. It also could be that you have solid educational expertise or years of experience with working professionally in one or more of these areas. This could allow you to be in another area of the music business that doesn't involve you singing or playing an instrument at all. This is where a hobby comes in. Sing or play music for a hobby and still enjoy that lesser talent you have while putting your money on your true strength that is worthy of building a business on. This is where you have to be "brutally honest" with yourself early on.

Build a business on the skills and talents for which people are already drawn to you professionally, not simply what you think you would like to be known for in life. God gives each of us at least one solid talent or gifting, so you need to identify yours before you start to build a business.

You can choose a field of pursuit, but you have little choice when it comes to your strengths and what you are really good at. So much of this is given by God at birth and needs to be exercised repeatedly to take it to a higher and higher level. If you don't yet know "what you're best at," ask your family, close friends, those you formerly worked for, and those you currently work with. They can help you quickly identify your strengths with precision.

One of the best ways I have found to measure passion in a business owner is by way of energy. If you have high energy around a particular subject, talent, or the business itself, it is almost a sure thing that you have planted yourself in the middle of your passion. This is one reason that business owners are often known for working long hours. Many times their positions require it to keep all of the plates spinning and to get their businesses up and off the ground. But the business owner is often so passionate about what they are doing and working toward that they have what seems like boundless energy to continue in the pursuit of building it and making it better.

When it comes to predicting success, I'll take passion and desire over talent any day. If you have enough passion, you will be able to persist to overcome most every difficulty and set back imaginable. If you are wise enough to couple your gifting with passion and persistence over a long period of time, you become almost unstoppable.

Take the time on the front end to do whatever it takes to ensure that you are building a business that really fits who you are and what you love. Doing this will give you the best chance of not only producing the highest level of financial success, but also the highest level of true satisfaction from your life's work. Having a passion for your business also will end up being the best sales tool you will ever have to offer. Once people see that you really love what you do, and believe in it from deep within, it will be easy to sell your product or service. It simply becomes a natural extension of who you are and what you love.

Successful business owner: if you honestly admit that your passion has dried up, and your enjoyment and fulfillment are running low, it is time to step back long enough to make a true assessment of where you are. No matter what phase of life you are in or what phase your business is in, it is never too late to adjust your sails and get back on course with who God created you to be. Life is too short to continue going down the wrong path. You are too valuable to our society not to be doing and producing what you were made to do. Don't continue to write off those feelings and prompts you have that tell you life should be more enjoyable and fulfilling. Take the time to talk to someone you trust who can assist you in making either the tweaks that are needed, or the major moves that may be necessary. Find your place and give the world who God made you to be. Your business needs to reflect this and here is where you have to start. I'm excited for you, whether this journey of building a business is a new one or whether it is an ever-growing adventure that keeps getting better and better.

CHAPTER 1:

CHAPTER CHALLENGE

1. Over the next three weeks, take at least an hour at a time to sit alone with a cup of coffee or a glass of iced tea, and a legal pad and pen. Think over your life from your years as a kid, all the way through this year, and write down the times in your life that stand out as the times you have enjoyed the most. Write exactly what you were doing, where you were, and who you were with at the time this joy came over you. Compile this list and look for common denominators from these experiences throughout your life to date. Highlight the common denominators.

2. Next, meet with at least two of your most trusted friends or family members and share this information with them. Ask them to give you feedback about what they are hearing. Also ask them about what they see as talents in any of these areas that might have assisted in leading to joy during these times and events.

3. Once you've recognized what you really love to do and the specific environments that give you the most pleasure, be sure that your business ideas (or your current business enterprise) incorporate several of these types of experiences that have given you the most joy over your lifetime. If this is not

the case, draw up a plan as to how you can redirect some of your business initiatives to incorporate the things and activities that you love. It may be as simple as making minor tweaks to your business plan (or your current business enterprise), or it may be as complex as making major overhauls.

Whatever the case, if you currently own your own business, make the move while also taking the advice of other business professionals such as your C.P.A. and banker. You want to make these changes in a way that does not disrupt your cash flow and profitability. Some major changes may need to be made very slowly over a long period of time to prevent any negative impacts to your business. Even if this is the case, it will give you great satisfaction to know that you are at least heading in the right direction for your heart. The end result can lead you not only to have greater financial success, but to a fulfillment of your calling in life.

You probably will find that what you love to do is also something that you are really good at as well. Expertise must be coupled with passion to have true success; usually joy comes from being exceptional at a particular skill or field of endeavor. Advice from respected professionals can keep you from trying to make a profession out of a hobby that you are not accomplished in. If you take your time and obtain the appropriate advice, you will find the balance that can increase your joy, while also raising your level of profit in a business.

CHAPTER 2:

LEARN THE ROPES
AND "GIVE ME 10"

A second common practice of successful business owners is that they learn the ropes of their particular industry by making mistakes while working for someone else first. Most start-up small businesses with fewer than two years of tenure don't have the excess capital to afford costly mistakes. Therefore, it is imperative that they hit the ground running with as much previous "like" experience as possible when they are funding on their own dime.

This is certainly not to say that business owners should try to make mistakes working for another company so that they can benefit from more lessons learned. Most mature businesses, though, have enough guard rails in place to keep employee mistakes from wreaking havoc on the company's cash flow. This, of course, is not the case when you run your own business. One big mistake (or a series of smaller ones) can bring a quick end to your career as a business owner.

Having a few years of experience in your chosen field before embarking on business ownership will certainly increase your chances of success. Once you've seen the lay of the land and learned how to maneuver through the most common challenges of your field, you are positioned to be a much more efficient and effective owner of your business.

For example, I conducted banking for several years for an industrial installation and service company. The two owners, one strong in sales and the other strong in administration and finance, had worked together previously at a large company in this same industry for approximately 15 years each. (Partnering with and hiring people who compliment a business owner's weaker areas is another lesson these individuals could teach, but more on that later.) The two partners received a first-class education in their field while getting paid for it. They also were patient enough while working for someone else to save a lot of cash to buffer them through any tough times with their own business.

The owners were able to take along their knowledge of the best processes of their previous employer while making notes of what could be improved if they were calling the shots. These two partners slowly, and in a calculated way, built up cash reserves, acquired equipment and vehicles at bargain prices, and laid the framework for their business.

Additionally, the owners were able to connect with other workers in their industry whose work they respected. These workers were certainly top on their list when it came time to hire their initial staff that would make or break their business. It was imperative that they have a strong team of horses to pull the initial load and build the momentum for the future life of their business.

This particular business took off like a locomotive and their profitability rose to great heights in quick fashion. However, this was all predicated upon the years of experience and expertise that these two owners had built when no one was watching. As the Bible says, "Whatever a person sows he will also reap" (Galatian 6:7, CSB). When a business takes off like a rocket and becomes exceptionally profitable within a brief period of time, there is always a depth of expertise and experience that has been sewn behind the scenes. There truly is no easy way to the top; every person must pay their dues one way or the other. Just like a future star athlete, a highly successful business owner must pay a lot of dues with training "in the gym" while no one is watching, and while he or she is only learning the ropes. No wise person starts out on the high rope unless they have spent time learning how to walk on a rope that is close to the ground. This way they can fall off, get back on, fall off, and get back on again before the price of falling or making mistakes is too costly.

Certainly, no professional singer, athlete, or dancer would ever want to give a performance before a packed auditorium or stadium without a good, solid warm up. In the same way, it makes no sense to place your life savings on the line, along with the reputation of your new business venture, without doing a lengthy test run in the same industry while working for someone else. It is always better to take a test ride with the training wheels on before balancing on two wheels with nothing but the wisdom and skill sets you've acquired between your right and left ears.

An additional benefit of working in your industry of choice before being an owner is that you learn the players in that industry and they learn you. You discover which vendors and service providers do the best work. You find out who has a reputation of gold and who are the "sharks" in your particular part of the "ocean." This time in the saddle also allows you to develop strong relationships with others in the industry who can be instrumental to your success.

A final benefit can be that you give yourself time to develop a credible reputation among peers. These peers can bless you with referrals of certain pieces of business due to the trust they have built in your ability and commitment to get the job done and to get it done right.

Your competitor may be a referral source if a particular project doesn't fit well into their wheelhouse. They might prefer to hand an opportunity to you rather than leave a referral they received with no options. Therefore, it is good for you to establish what specific part of your industry at which you are the best, or what service or product that you deliver better than anyone else. For instance, a general mechanic may often refer a transmission rebuild or replacement to a particular business that specializes in this unique service, just as a dentist might refer a patient to an oral surgeon to have their wisdom teeth removed. Building a solid reputation in your field on the front end can have various benefits when you become the business owner. Some of these benefits may surprise you and not be visible until you've been in the driver's seat of your own company for a few months or years.

Here's the bottom line: Be wise enough to let experienced fishermen and fisherwomen teach you how to fish before you grab the rod and reel. Much money and time can be saved when you learn from others who were there sooner and have been there longer than you. And trust me, when it is your dollar that is being saved by making smarter decisions the first time, the pay-off hits close to home.

The second part of my advice from this chapter sounds like that of a Marine drill sergeant: "Give me 10!" Normally these words would conjure a vision of seeing a private removing his or her hat and doing a quick set of 10 pushups. This is not exactly the image I had in mind. Actually, the exercise is much more difficult (and fun, if you are in a career field that is a good fit for you). To clarify, "Give me 10 years!" Yes, 10 years.

It is a well-accepted fact that you can become an expert in almost anything in life with 10 years of experience and training— an expert physician, lawyer, teacher, singer, dancer, and so forth. Ten years—there is something magical about that number. It is truly amazing what can be accomplished in a decade of focused study and application. One can go from a complete novice to a credentialed expert within this time period. One can go from a complete unknown in a particular field to being renown in that same field within this time period. If you live to be 80 and own your own business for 30 or more years, would it not make sense to invest at least an initial 10 solid years building your expertise in your chosen life's work?

I realize that may be asking too much for those of you who are filled with passion, confidence, and energy to start a business and light the world on fire. If you can't "give me 10," at least commit to give 5 years of your life to thoroughly learn your field of choice before launching into the deep unknown with your life savings and your future on the line. The more time you spend on the front-end learning from others who are experts, the more sure-footed you will be when you are the one calling the shots and reaping the rewards or the consequences of your actions. I'm not asking you for perfection—just a reasonable amount of preparation, because a lot is on the line. Be gutsy, but don't be foolish.

One thing is for sure: The respect commanded by being an expert is well worth the time taken to acquire this credential. It also tends to pay off in revenue volume. If I go to a new chiropractic practice, would I be comfortable allowing someone to adjust my spine if they had only been in their field for one year? Or would I be much more willing to trust my vertebrae to someone who has acquired not only the proper training, but also has learned the ropes working for another practice under a more experienced chiropractor for several years.

Most people value experience and expertise when it comes to the important things, such as the care of their own body, their time, and ... their *money*. As a current or future business owner, give your clients a real reason to spend their hard-earned money on your product or services: You have taken no shortcuts on training and experience in order to offer them the most professional and efficient service possible.

Let me share an experience I had with a gentleman who started a tree service company and ran it for over three decades. This business owner founded his company out of a lifelong interest in trees and woodland environments. Over time, he collected many certifications related to his industry. Upon speaking with this business owner, it becomes apparent very quickly that he has spent most of his lifetime learning, obtaining an education, and growing through decades of experience in the knowledge of how best to care for trees of all kinds.

Before having some trees cut down in our backyard, I interviewed three companies. While all of the companies were certainly capable of getting the job done, there was no comparison to the knowledge and expertise of one company over the other two. While this company was not the least expensive, their pricing was reasonable, and I was willing to pay a little more for the expertise, care, and experience that this one company was able to provide. In addition, I eventually recommended this company to others who had similar needs.

So you see, this gentleman's willingness to take the time to learn and perfect his craft over the long haul paid off with multiple opportunities for business from just one person—me. Imagine how many times this scenario has probably been repeated through many people who have recognized and appreciated his expertise and long-term dedication to his craft. There is no doubt that taking the time to build it right does pay off for your business.

Another question to ponder: If you don't enjoy what you're doing enough to be committed to learning and mastering it for at least 10 years, are you in the correct field? Is this really an endeavor in which you want to invest most of your money, time, and energy with no guarantee of a quick return or immediate way out? In the ebbs and flows of our economy, I have noticed that it tends to be the "long-termers" who continually make it through the down times and come out whole on the other side. The timid, less-committed players are the first to jump ship when the grass *seems* greener in another pasture. Which do you want to be: a mainstay or a runaway?

When it comes to presenting yourself and your company to prospective clients, there is no substitute for high-caliber training and "stick-to-it" tenure. It commands immediate respect and does more to enhance your selling skills than the President's Club training course at the Sandler Sales Institute (though I have benefitted from this program and recommend it as well). If you are the "real deal" and have paid your dues, you don't have to cower to anyone and you can say with full confidence that you can deliver what you promise. You literally will have "been there, done that," even if you weren't the "boss" at the time. If you "give me 10," or at least "5," you can shoot straight with your prospects and they will know you are the "real deal."

I also can vouch for the value of tenure in my own line of work. After I obtained my BBA in Finance from Belmont University in Nashville, Tennessee, I spent part of two years on a political finance team and 25 years working in various positions for a total of four banks. In addition, I graduated from two Tennessee Bankers' Association schools of banking and took additional college coursework to expand my expertise. Over this long tenure, I developed experience working in almost every facet of the banking industry. This wealth of experience and know-how allowed me the opportunity to become a Market President for the last three banks for which I have worked. I share this information simply to let you know that I practice what I preach and I believe it enough to live it.

The bottom line: Don't short-cut yourself, your business, or your future clients by gaining anything less than a strong, tenured resume in your field of choice *before* you become the captain of the ship. In the long run, it will save you a lot of money, a lot of time, and a lot of good will among your client base. If you want to be a true leader in your field, there are no real short-cuts. However, with the proper investment and commitment of yourself, the payoff can be tremendous.

CHAPTER 2:

CHAPTER CHALLENGE

1. For the field of endeavor you want to pursue for a business, list all of the training, years of work experience, and significant accomplishments you have achieved in and around this chosen field. Name any professional certifications or awards that you have received related to this field. After making the list, step away from it. Then try to objectively ask: If you were looking to hire a person to run a business in this field, would you hire yourself given your current background, level of expertise, and accomplishments in this industry?

2. Next, show this list to two or three key friends who have expertise in business and ask them the same question to see if they really think you are qualified to start or lead this venture.

3. If you find you are lacking (even if you have already got your business moving in full swing), construct a list of additional training and experiences that could help bolster your background and assist you in becoming more of an expert in your field. Be sure to list seminars, formal education, books to read, mentorships, and any other additional items or ideas that could help you build more background

and expertise in order to propel your business forward and to give you an edge in your industry.

Be honest enough with yourself and ask your friends to be honest enough with you to let you know if you really possess an extraordinary talent or expertise in a given field. When putting your whole financial and professional future on the line, you want to be sure that you do it in the field in which you are truly gifted. If this is not the case, it is better to learn early and admit it, than to go blindly into a profession at which you never were that great in the first place.

Everyone has a gifting and you need to find yours and be sure you have allowed this gifting to "season" with the proper amount of experience, training, and practice to allow it to really shine. If you and your friends don't see concrete evidence of this in your chosen field or business, it is time to evaluate if you are in the right area and what needs to be done to maximize your chances of success in a particular type of business.

This works just as well for a business owner who is already well down the road in years of business ownership. It allows the owner to take a good, honest look at how qualified and talented they are, while also evaluating what can be done to make them better in their chosen field. It also shows how updated and on the cutting edge that he or she is in their field.

If your training and education about your field are dated, then are you due or overdue for an update? Never be afraid to ask yourself these tough questions.

It is better for you to ask these questions, no matter what stage of the process you are in, than for you to find out too late that you really don't have the resources necessary to oversee a successful business in that industry. Always be courageous enough to ask yourself the hard questions first. Then you will receive the right answers and you also will have the courage to ask others in your business the hard questions, when needed, to be sure that your business achieves the maximum success possible.

CHAPTER 3:

STAY IN LINE

I once heard a preacher tell his congregation to "stay in line" as a way of life. He counseled them on the benefits of staying in the one line you are in, even when the lines to your left or right seem to be moving faster. That preacher said that if you stay in the line you are in, you will keep moving toward the front and you eventually will end up at the front of the line. However, if you keep getting out of line to move to another line that "seems" to be moving faster, you always will remain in transition and you never will get to the front of the line. I couldn't agree more.

Let me explain. The most successful business owners I know have been in their respective fields from 20- to 40-plus years. They've been in that industry through many up-and-down cycles and they have learned how to ride the wave and endure. They know their industry inside and out, because they have stayed focused on one particular field for many years. It is true that there is no substitute for experience. A knowledge base gained from years of practice gives one the ability to stand strong, while other less-tenured leaders waver under the pressures that always come at some time in business.

If I consider lending money to help a business grow, I want to know without a doubt that the business owner is fully committed to their business and the industry. When the storms come, I know I will find this type of person scooping the water out of their boat and fighting for survival because she or he is "all in."

As a side note, you may have noticed that I say "he or she" in many references. I have had the pleasure of working with many female C.E.O.s, physicians, C.P.A.s, and so forth, who have a tremendous talent for running their businesses. I am glad to say that the "good ol' boy" network is long out of style. I tip my hat to the many women who have created successful businesses from which we all have benefitted.

I also have noticed that many efficiencies are gained when a business owner stays on focus in his or her particular industry. Medical offices run smoother, roofing contractors control costs better, and legal firms generate more billable hours as they hone their skill in a specific field without stepping outside their area of expertise.

On the other hand, I've seen many business owners who jump from one field to another every few years, and frankly, that scares me. I have to ask myself if I am keeping someone's savings safe when I am loaning it, through the bank, to a person who has a "curvy" track record. If the owner doesn't stay long in one field, then what makes me think he or she will have the commitment or the know-how to weather the storms that someday will hit their business? You can't help but respect a long, consistently straight track record, and you can't help but question a choppy, non-committed one. With every consistent track record there exists a person who has fought through tough times and challenges, unexpected valleys, and unfair situations to come out stronger on the other side with their head still held high. This is the kind of leader I want with me when things don't go as planned down the road.

I realize that not everyone out there can have a 30-year track record, especially when you've only been in business for two years. But you can head in that direction with a simple choice: stay in line. No matter how long the line, you eventually will get to the front if you will stay in the same line. The alternative is that you can spend your life jumping from line to line, industry to industry, and never become a line leader. You can spend all of your time, energy, and mental capacity learning the nuances of different industries, and never realize the level of mastery you can obtain by sticking with one trade. To put it another way, would you want to go to a brain surgeon who moonlights as a plumber and an electronics repairman? Or would you prefer a surgeon who uses all of her professional time and energy to keep her skills and knowledge to the highest possible level?

I am not suggesting that times and circumstances don't ever come to knock you out of line. There are definitely periods in the economy and other circumstances in life that may cause us to have to get out of line. Also, we may realize over time and years that we are simply standing in the wrong line and that it *is* better for us overall to move to another line. What I am saying is that we should not make a habit of switching lines and moving from thing to thing if we want to have true success in life.

There is a benefit that can only come through the perseverance of fighting through challenges, discouragements, and disappointments. You have to experience this type of resistance, and persevere through it to gain real success. If you keep jumping out of something before you warrior through this challenging period, you will never find true satisfaction in your work and business.

Remember those two Ps that every business owner should have posted in their board room: Passion and Persistence? If you want to add a third P, it should be Patience. Passion and Persistence can help you move up in the line you are in, and Patience can help you stay in your current line so you can reach the maximum position possible. Also, patience can help you stay in line when you are tempted to switch lines because another line (or industry or business) appears to be moving faster than the one you are in. You show me a business owner who has a healthy dose of Passion, Persistence, and Patience, and it is just a matter of time until something very good happens for this person and their company.

In today's hyper-competitive and fast-paced business landscape, being innovative and continually adapting to changing demands is absolutely necessary. While mastering your chosen field over time gives you a distinct advantage in business, you must balance this with continually changing the way you utilize technology and innovation to satisfy the always-changing tastes of your customer base. No one can be highly successful by doing the same thing the same way for years on end without adaptation. Keep the long-term commitment to developing expertise and practicing living out your values, while embracing change on a daily basis. This combination will give you the balance to continue to lead the pack both now and in the future.

You also must be careful not to allow your greatest strength to become your greatest weakness. Staying with your business and your field long-term always must be balanced with wisdom and common sense. In today's rapidly changing business environment, many thriving businesses today will not be needed two, three, or five years from now.

Who would have thought that the demand for VHS movies and cassette tapes in the 80s would have gone to zero in the age of DVDs and CDs? Or that the demand for DVDs and CDs would have gone to zero in the age of streaming and downloads? There is much wisdom and strength in sticking with something, but you also must be able to be honest enough with yourself to admit when something is no longer working or when your product/service is no longer in demand. Even with constantly rolling changes, there is a huge benefit for consistency and for staying close to what you really know.

Let me share a simple, yet profound, principle from a true story about my grandfather, Altus Robert Bennett. Mr. A.R., as the people in my hometown of Ila, Georgia called him, was an agriculture teacher, high school principal, farmer, and business owner. He spent most of his life as an educator, and later in retirement as a school board member. My grandfather's passion was educating his students about life from the agriculture classes he taught during the week, to the Sunday School class he led on Sunday mornings.

When my grandfather taught agriculture back in the 1950's, his class began to discuss the destructive work of the boll weevil. The boll weevil was a new threat to cotton and all crop farmers at this time; many crops were destroyed in the late 1950's by this small insect. A young man in class asked my grandfather: "Mr. Bennett, since the boll weevil is so destructive, should we consider another career besides crop farming?" My grandfather looked at him and replied "Son, there will be boll weevils in anything you go into." What a true statement!

Each worthy field of endeavor will have its boll weevils, challenges, and frustrations. But the farmer who sticks with his chosen field (no pun intended) will reap the benefits and efficiencies of focused experience, and will find ways to overcome the "boll weevils." He or she will produce an even greater crop through the experience.

Those farmers who got out of farming when the boll weevils hit missed the rewards that came when the boll weevil was finally extinguished. In the same way, those who spend their energy getting in and out of lines miss the benefits and rewards of becoming an expert in their field. It may take a while to get to the front of the line, but oh, is it worth it!

Innovation, a very necessary component of success, becomes much easier when you thoroughly know your product or service through years of experience. Creatively persevering through the trials that come your way bestows many blessings on your business and your personal life that sometimes only can be seen in hindsight.

The better you get at something, the more fun it becomes. I love to watch the skill of a highly-trained dentist performing a root canal (as long as it's not on me), or seeing the long-time owner of an antique business make a quick (but accurate) appraisal on a piece of furniture that was just shown to them. There's just something special about excellence in any field. No matter the industry, no matter the specialty, it is always invigorating to watch. And...do you know how you get it? You "stay in line."

Besides sticking with one type of business and one industry for a long time, it pays to see people not get too far out of their area of expertise with side ventures and investments. It is truly hard to master multiple fields. I've watched many professionals who were experts in their field learn the hard way that their expertise in one field does not easily transfer to a completely different field.

Because you are a really good physician does not mean you will be a good real estate developer. Because you are a good stockbroker does not mean you will be a good company C.F.O. Each particular field has its own unique challenges and must be respected for these. It can be financially dangerous to assume that mastery of one field will give you the skill set necessary to master another, completely different field. A lot of us may be good at several things, but normally one thing really stands out and this is what you can build a career on. The other lesser talents are better left as hobbies, in my opinion.

Again, the "stay in line" principle applies. When a physician tells me he or she wants to begin to develop commercial office buildings, it makes me nervous. Many with this mindset are heading for disaster and financial ruin. They often leave their "cash cow" of medicine to practice at developing real estate. Before long, the practice cash flow suffers because they begin to devote more time to their newfound passion, at which they are much less efficient than the practice of medicine. It doesn't take long to discover they have missed efficiencies that would have been realized by a true, seasoned real-estate developer. Often, they also have fallen into unseen pitfalls that professionals in the real estate industry would have seen far enough in advance to avoid.

Do any of us really think we can transfer into something new and perform like a 25-year pro, no matter how smart we are? Sound business wisdom once again tells us to "stay in line" and stick with what we know best. Then with the money we make from our own "cash cow," we can pay someone to perform other work for us or invest for us and take advantage of the long time that they have spent "in line," learning and perfecting their craft.

It is interesting and enlightening to see the courage that is developed in a business owner who has weathered through past storms. Fighting and being courageous in the face of difficulties and over-coming obstacles renders a confidence that cannot be obtained any other way. It is thrilling for me to watch a seasoned business owner deal with a particularly challenging event occurring with their business. I like to see the confidence and skill they have in planning how they will survive and thrive in spite of the challenge. They don't consider backing down or letting it beat them. They take it as a challenge and thrive on being tested, because they know they have been down a similar road before and have won.

As a business owner, you can't be afraid to fight. Whether you like it or not, the fight will come to you at some time in the life of your business. It also may come to you many times during the ownership of your company. Economic cycles always will rise and fall every few years, technology will continually evolve, consumer tastes will change, competition will arise when you least expect it, and so on. Though you may run the same business for years, it will not be boring because the environment in which you operate your business will constantly change and challenge you in different ways.

As I write this book, businesses are still dealing with some of the challenges of the COVID-19 Pandemic. Businesses that thrive through this time and continue to maintain profitability will have to continually innovate and modify the way they do business. This would be an easy time for business owners to bail out, but where would that leave them? There are ways to innovate, persevere, and find new opportunities for generating revenue even in the COVID-19 environment.

Business owners who know their industry best will find ways to continue to thrive. They also will be able to take the current obstacles as a challenge to see how they can be creative and courageous in the face of uncertainty. They will stay "in line," stay encouraged, and they will find a way through this challenge. Additionally, they understand that the pressure and struggles brought on from this current economic challenge will make them better, stronger, and faster if they endure. Therefore, a business owner can become excited when the heat is on, knowing it will force them to step it up and come out even better in the long run.

Owning your own business is definitely not for cowards and not for those who run from a fight or a challenge. Being successful in your business requires a lot of tenacity and grit that enables you to "stay in line." This tenacity will eventually get you to the front of the line where your business and your picture will be the one on the front page of the newspaper. At that time, you will be glad you paid the price for the success that you know you've earned.

CHAPTER 3:

CHAPTER CHALLENGE

1. List how many years you have invested in your chosen profession. How much education and training do you have in this field? How old were you when you became interested in this field and how dedicated have you been to this chosen profession to date? Is there one field that stands out above all others in which your talent lies, or are you multi-talented and have you succeeded some in many different areas in your life to date?

2. Do you find yourself waking each day with excitement about what you will learn and accomplish in this chosen field, or has it been a career in which you have had to push yourself to stay involved and stay focused? Do you believe you are gifted in this particular field of endeavor? Do you sense somewhat of a "calling" that this is your way of giving back to others through your service in this particular industry? Do you have a vision for how you can benefit people's lives long-term through this type of business?

3. Remember that staying with one field long enough to become one of the best at it will take many years of tenacity. Are you sure you have what it takes to last through these challenges and still come

out swinging? It will take more than simple will-power, and you need to consider the cost prior to jumping in.

If you are already in a particular business or industry, the sooner you can assess your overall level of long-term commitment, the better. Don't be afraid to challenge your level of commitment by looking back at what you have done to date.

Be honest enough with yourself to question whether you have the passion and expertise for what you are doing to be able to continue this for another 10, 20, or more years. To be the best you have to be committed to work through challenges, grow through ups and downs, never give up, and love what you do enough to do it over and over again. Do you have what it takes to "stay in line" in the business you are currently in for many years to come? Knowing the answer to this question will give you freedom to make the best decisions for you and your business. The truth eventually will come out anyway, so the sooner you know and acknowledge the truth, the more preparation time you will have to make any changes that are needed.

CHAPTER 4:

GROW SLOW

It never pays to be in a hurry when making financial decisions. It also never pays to be in a hurry when growing your business. With growth comes increased risk, need for additional capital, loss of control, and many other challenges that can capsize even the most successful business. Therefore, it pays to take it slow. If adding a location increases profit, then it makes sense to add two more locations next year, right? Not necessarily. If your revenues grew last year from $1 million to $2 million, then it is wise to try to double your growth again in the next two years, right? Again, not necessarily. Navigating the waters of a business can change drastically with increased growth, particularly if that growth is dramatic.

Growing a successful business is like growing your personal wealth; it is usually more successful when it is done little by little, in baby steps. Overseeing a larger budget, more employees, and a larger territory, plus dealing with more regulations and compliance requirements is difficult to take on at a fast pace. Slowly expanding your areas of oversight and responsibility gives you more time to develop your expertise and skill so that you keep putting your best foot forward.

Some calculated risks are necessary and come with the territory of being a business owner. However, large amounts of risk brought on by huge growth spurts can just as easily put you into bankruptcy as it can put you in a mansion on the hill. Increasing the debt on a business in rapid fashion to keep up with skyrocketing sales often can come crashing down on you when you experience a bump in the road, consumer tastes change, technology changes, or the overall market changes. It is important to coordinate with your C.P.A. and banker to determine the proper amount of financial leverage that will keep your business growing, while still enabling you to withstand unexpected challenges and turns in the market.

Any type of fixed cost that you add to your business (a cost that must be paid, no matter what your level of production, revenue, or profit) puts a higher demand and pressure on the resources of your business. It also puts a higher level of stress on you personally as a business owner. Just as bridges and dams were only made to withstand a certain amount of pressure at one time, your business always will have limits each year as to the amount of borrowing or accruing debt that it can reasonably service. All fixed costs, such as additional full-time employees, payments on equipment, buildings, commercial vehicles, rent, or insurance premiums, set the bar higher and higher that must be achieved to end up with a profit each month, quarter, and year. A wise business owner will think long-term before adding these types of costs to ensure that they don't become an unnecessary and troublesome burden to their business.

A business owner needs to decide over time how much is enough in relation to income, lifestyle, and size of the business. High growth does not always equate to high profit and large wealth. For some business owners, the worst thing that ever happened was to drastically increase their sales through having their products distributed through a major retailer.

This type of growth, for instance, can decrease control because now 70 percent of the revenue may come from one customer. This gives that large retailer the power to come back and demand lower prices, which in turn can drastically reduce the profit that the small business owner realizes on each unit of product they produce. In the meantime, the business owner may have hired more employees, rented more space, purchased more machinery, and borrowed heavily on a line of credit to keep up with this sudden increase in demand for their product. The business owner quickly can find themselves simply trying to stay above water because they now have all of these fixed costs, yet their profit margins are being squeezed.

At best, this could be an incredibly stressful time for the owner as she or he works through this season until they can diversify their customer base once again. At worst, this situation eventually could cause this business to go into bankruptcy. I have seen this type of scenario too many times simply because a business owner refused to check their ego and keep things slow and steady. Many business owners have forged ahead with taking on a breakneck pace of growth, only to look back a year or two and long for the simplicity, control, and profitability when the business was smaller and more manageable. While growth is not necessarily bad, be sure it is the right kind of growth, for the right reasons, at a reasonable and sustainable pace for both you and your business.

In my banking career to date, I have worked with many professionals in dentistry. This includes general dentists, orthodontists, periodontists, endodontists, oral surgeons, and pediatric dentists. I have seen some of these dental professionals build a single practice that sustained them and their families with solid income. At the same time, just having one practice allowed them to maintain a life balance that gave them enough time to be at their children's ball games, be home in time for dinner with their family, have some time to relax on the weekend, and have an overall blessed life.

On the other hand, I have watched as some dental professionals grew to open more locations, hire additional staff, make more money, and become entrenched in the "machine" they created. I also have witnessed some dental professionals who grew their one practice to multiple practices and, because they were spread so thin, they actually made less money than other dental professionals who ran a single, focused practice.

Am I saying that growth is wrong and that the desire to grow your business, whatever industry you are in, is wrong and always fraught with problems? No, I would never say that on a universal basis. But I will say that seeking tremendous growth is often at the root of a lot of very unhappy people who would have been much better off to simply keep a steady pace.

I have often seen that the motivation behind growing a business to dizzying heights is built upon ego or the lack of self-acceptance, and not on sound business principles. Meaning: I have seen some business owners who try to grow a business too fast and push the pace too much in order to compensate for personal feelings of inferiority that will never be satisfied, no matter how large and successful their business becomes. If these entrepreneurs don't deal with their underlying insecurities, life will result in a bankrupt business, a broken marriage, or children who don't even really know them. There is a reason that the Bible says: "For the love of money is the root of all kinds of evil" (1 Timothy 6:10, CSB).

Be sure you are courageous enough to face the motivations that drive you, and humble enough to admit when you are off course. This can make the difference between long-term success and a life of ultimate failure brought on by an ego and drive that went off track.

I suggest that you view debt in your business as a servant and a master. An appropriate amount of debt can give your business the lift it needs to grow and become more valuable over time. However, when the amount of debt that you take on crosses the line and becomes excessive, it can be a harsh task master that will run your business, your personal life, and your health into the ground. So be adventurous and bold, but also be humble and thankful for where you are so that you achieve a solid balance that will pay off in the long run.

When I was a college student at Belmont University in Nashville, Tennessee, there was a statue on campus of a businessman that had his foot on a large dollar sign. The statue was named "Servant or Master?" In life, we are allowed to choose whether money, success, and business growth become our *servant* or our *master*. Money can be a wonderful servant and can be used to help a lot of people. But it is a terrible master that will suck the life out of you if you let it.

There is another important question to ask yourself as a business owner: Do you want to have the satisfaction of having a tight rein on your business? It can allow you to keep all of your service standards at a particular level and allow you to be "hands on." It will provide the touch that made your business successful in the first place.

Or are you the type of business owner who wants to start up an enterprise? You enjoy growing it to a certain extent, then either selling it to someone else to take it to the next level or bringing in a lot of other talent who can oversee tremendous expansion while you accept less and less control.

One thing is for certain—You only have so much time, energy, knowledge, and ability. Therefore, you must make a decision related to the areas and game plan that you will focus on with your business. You will find it impossible to maintain a tight grip on your business while also experiencing tremendous growth. In a different way, you will find it equally impossible to keep your fingerprints all over your business, while at the same time expecting it to grow to tremendous heights. Some of these answers will come from your personality, some from your talents, and still others from your desires and what gives you true satisfaction.

Many business owners derive much pleasure in building large companies that can employ and provide for thousands of people and their families. These owners enjoy making this impact. Others obtain more satisfaction from employing a few people with whom they've become close enough to call family. They take pride in the fact that nothing is done or produced at their company without the utmost attention to detail and without a careful, watchful eye to ensure that every client is satisfied to the utmost.

Exploring these differences can help you determine if you should build a large business for the masses or a small business that can make more direct impact on fewer people. While there is no right or wrong answer, the important task is to choose which is the right fit for you and the lifestyle you desire.

While it is not guaranteed that you will have the ability or the option to build a large business, it is highly recommended that you know going into your business what type of lifestyle and oversight will truly bring you contentment and happiness. Whatever you decide, growing slow will enable you to make adjustments if you begin to see things that make you uncomfortable or cause you heartburn.

"Slow and steady" sets you on a growth path with your business upon which you can consistently make the changes and adaptations that keep things from getting off track and going down the wrong road. With this type of business plan, you will have the option to make the tweaks necessary to keep the road smooth and not "outrun your headlights." A business moving forward at a frantic pace often will not allow such actions and quickly can get out of control. It can cause you to run as fast as you can chasing your business, instead of diligently leading it toward the path you want it to follow.

Remember, everything that glitters is not gold. Determine what is required to make you happy and set the parameters accordingly. If family time is most important, don't sacrifice it for growth in your business. If making a decent living with less stress is a priority, don't put yourself in a growth pattern that will demand intensive travel along with a crazy amount of hours. Once you turn the speed up, it is difficult to slow it down and you quickly can find yourself on a treadmill that you can't turn off.

On the other hand, if you slowly turn up the growth of your business, you give yourself the time to adjust and to determine if this is a comfortable fit for you, and if it's where you want to be. Slow growth gives you the ability to set limits and maintain control.

If you determine that you want to take things up another notch, you still have that option. Doing so is a better long-term approach; I have found that most business owners never regret going this route. Real wealth, financial freedom, and joy in your chosen profession and industry is not found in a few years of intense growth. It is found through many years of maintaining balance in your life and your business. In the long run, the tortoise beats the hare, and still has time to stop and smell some roses while doing it.

CHAPTER 4:

CHAPTER CHALLENGE

1. If you have not done so at this point, write a business plan for your business. If the business is already established and running, this plan can be for the next five to ten years to shine light on what you want to accomplish and how you want to grow and thrive. The plan should cover everything from product or service differentiation and innovation, to marketing, analysis of the competition, and financial projections for the future from the best information you currently have on hand.

2. If you are beginning your business, speak with industry experts and gain knowledge through your chosen industry's trade associations. This can supply you with financial information applicable to similar businesses in your field. You can gain knowledge about average profit margins, fixed costs, capital requirements, average accounts receivable and accounts payable turn times, and so forth. These can be helpful in making financial projections and planning how you will sustain your business until it gets up and running, and producing a profit.

   You also can engage a C.P.A. or an attorney, or work with organizations such as the Small Business Association (SBA) or Service Corps of Retired

Executives (SCORE) to gain knowledge and wisdom to help you with your business plan and to provide continued guidance. The SBA and SCORE offer many services for free, so don't neglect to check out these offerings.

3. Along with a business plan, think through and record your thoughts, hopes, and desires for the size of business you want to own or grow, the amount of control you want to keep on the day-to-day running of the business, and the amount of time you are willing to devote to your business. Hopefully, when you determine the amount of time you are willing to put into your business, you also look at the other areas of your life to include family time, your faith or spiritual life, and time for relaxation and hobbies. Remember, as my mother often told me, "all work and no play makes Jack a dull boy."

   In considering the size and amount of control you want over your business, be sure to consider your personality, your need for validation, and your priorities in relation to financial rewards.

   - How important is it to you that you are one of the "big dogs" in your industry or city?
   - How important is it to you to live in one of the largest houses in town?
   - How important is it to you to make it to the top of the hill?
   - How competitive are you?

Be honest with yourself when it comes to things such as dreams, ego, drive, and control. It is better to acknowledge who you are and how you are made than to act like someone you are not. Once this is determined, you can work with a mentor or friend to adjust the things you see that are not what you want to build your life on long-term. You always can modify your dreams once you have a clear vision of what they are.

CHAPTER 5:

NETWORK
AND PROMOTION

There is no substitute for building relationships one person at a time. If you build those relationships when you don't need them, you'll find they will be a lifesaver when you do have a need. Every person you get to know has their own circle of influence, which includes family, friends, and business associates.

The people in your sphere of influence can make a huge difference in the growth of your business over time. No matter what business you are in, a lot of success boils down to who you know and who knows you. The best place to start building your allies and your sphere of influence is in your local community where you live. This base of relationships can support you as you grow your influence to a larger audience.

As a business owner, you should identify two community-based organizations within your town or city in which you can serve. Find two organizations for which you have a passion and can enjoy being a part of over the next year or longer. One of those organizations could be a traditional group such as Rotary Club, Kiwanis Club, or Chamber of Commerce. Another good fit is any type of nonprofit group, such as one that helps the homeless, the poor, or victims of domestic abuse. In addition, an organization that caters to one of your favorite hobbies can be a great way to meet new people and expand your sphere of influence. Clubs and organizations exist that support fly-fishing, duck hunting, collecting exotic cars or motorcycles, making and enjoying music, and almost every activity imaginable.

By serving in these kinds of organizations, you can build solid relationships with other influencers in your community, while also helping to promote a good cause or hobby. Inevitably, when you get to know people in your community by serving together for a common cause, you end up doing business together. You learn respect for each other and for what you do for a living. It is always helpful to have other people in your community who can vouch for your integrity, work ethic, and expertise when people are inquiring about your business. Also, it is an even further benefit when other professionals and business owners can refer people to you for the services and products you provide because of their high level of respect for you.

Advertising, marketing, and direct selling can drive many customers your way. However, referrals from others is the residual gift that keeps on giving. Receiving consistent referrals each year from your centers of influence (COIs) often can be the best (and most counted on) sources for driving your sales revenue. As you build relationships with not only customers, but also other influencers, you can spend more of your time on innovating and improving your products and services, and less time on creating demand for them.

It is also advisable to develop a brief synopsis of what your business provides in plain, everyday language that everyone can understand. When you share this synopsis with everyone you meet, you provide a short and simple way for them to remember what you do, in case they or a friend or business associate need that type of service.

When telling people about your business and checking to see if they have a need, remember that a "no" may mean "maybe later." You sow seeds each day, week, month, and year that will reap rewards in the future, if you keep building your expertise and never give up. A Bible verse comes to mind: "Let us not get tired of doing good, for we will reap at the proper time if we don't give up" (Galatians 6:9, CSB). That advice has been around for a very long time, and it is still as true today as it was when it was written.

If you put your blood, sweat, and tears into building your business, as well as tons of work hours and your own money, you might as well become a walking, talking billboard for your company. While you don't have to spout facts about your business constantly and bore people to death, you always can be proud enough of the work you do to share a brief detail about how you can help people. You can hand them a card, tell them in 10 seconds what you do or make, and let them know that if you can ever be of service to them, you would love to do so.

You should never apologize for sharing your calling in life and offering to use your skills to help others. You also should never be ashamed of asking people for their business. You never will know until you ask, and you might be surprised to find that people are relieved to find someone like you (conscientious, friendly, hard-working, honest, skillful) who does what you do. All they can say is "no," which again, translated means "maybe later."

One of the real pleasures and opportunities of a business owner is that you can make a direct impact on your community through the influence you gain. It is a wonderful way to make life better in your community, while at the same time creating a positive public relations campaign for your commercial enterprise. Business owners who become involved in politics, helping those less fortunate, and assisting their communities in having a collective voice for the best of all citizens experience a fulfillment that surpasses simply running a business.

Knowing that you are influencing your community for the good and helping others is a wonderful fringe benefit for a business owner. Amazingly, when you do these great things for others, you can't help but show-case your business and receive positive public relations at the same time.

I have experienced this in my own career. I have worked to help students, faculty, and administrators in a large public high school in Nashville for many years. A woman introduced herself to me at a networking event, then informed me she had decided to move all of her personal and business banking services to me. She told me she was so impressed with how I handled myself and so appreciative of all I had done to help this particular high school, that she wanted me to be her banker. I was encouraged to hear these words. It helped me realize how much people watch what we do in our communities and our spheres of influence. We may not even know they are watching, but they are.

My efforts in helping this particular high school came from a calling that I felt to help these students. The majority of these students were from low-to-moderate income neighborhoods in which their parents often lacked higher education and often struggled financially.

I never looked at this mission as a PR move. Instead, I saw it as somewhat of a ministry in which I could utilize my influence in Nashville to help make this school better. I wanted to better the students who attended, the faculty who taught there, the administrators who led the school, and the many parents who had a desire to see their children benefit from a solid education.

However, it was interesting to see how many people and businesses were drawn to me as a potential banker through the activities I was involved in related to this school. They saw my leadership capabilities, my concern for our community, and how hard I was willing to work to make positive changes in a school that would affect our community. It was a great and unexpected benefit to gain business from this effort.

My advice is to do what you do to help and assist others for the right reason. But at the same time, don't be surprised when this effort yields more positive results back to you and your business than you ever planned. I look at it as a culmination of reaping what you sow.

Looking past any benefits that you may receive from building relationships with others and helping your community, city, and even state, it is also good to see the responsibility you have as a business owner. If you are "running the show" with your business, employing others, and benefiting financially from it, there is a certain responsibility you then have to use the power and influence you were given to help others.

My grandpa told me that "power is good as long as you use it to help people." Power and influence, if used for our own self-aggrandizement, is empty and unfulfilling. However, power that we obtain or are given, if used to help others (especially those less fortunate), provides a joy and sense of accomplishment that few things can rival.

Be sure not to miss out on this blessing that can come your way as a successful business owner. You have influence, your opinion matters, many people look up to you, and you can make a difference in many lives if you only take some time to try to do so.

In order to be a powerful networker and influencer for your business, you need to step out of your comfort zone and get to know others who may be different from you. You will benefit greatly from building relationships with people who have varied interests and beliefs, and who associate in different circles than you. Catering to one type of clientele only, can drastically limit your sphere of influence and business growth.

Join an organization, build close relationships with its members, and work your way up to serving on a committee or two. You eventually can sit on the board of directors, and possibly become an officer of the organization. Once you have completed this cycle, move on to another organization and do the same. This enables you to continually expand your sphere of influence, while keeping fresh by utilizing your skills and talents to help in a different environment and through a different cause.

I believe it is wise to continuously add to your contacts and to constantly build new relationships. After all, people you meet and get to know early in your business will grow older, possibly move, eventually retire, and some even will die. If you are not in the constant habit of continuing to reach out and build relationships with others, you will notice that your contacts and your sphere of influence will begin to contract over time.

As you age and your business grows, continue to create relationships with those who are younger than you. If you only focus on keeping up relationships with those who are your age and older, you will see a gradual reduction of your influence. Additionally, you often will miss out on learning new ways of keeping your business viable as times and seasons change.

For instance, if you are in your 50s, you should build relationships with those who are younger, as well as those your age and older. This not only helps to keep you fresh, relevant, and in touch with trends, attitudes, and technology, it just makes good economic sense for your business. You don't want your clients and contacts dying off with no way to replace them.

I absolutely love to see successful business owners in their 80s; quite a few are still energetic, passionate, and eager to learn. They get much of their energy and excitement from the fact that they are still improving, and are still making a difference in their business and community.

It is encouraging to watch this type of business owner speak to a room full of twenty-and thirty-some-thing-year-olds. They have so much passion and energy that they can still command the full attention of those who are much younger. While building relationships and seeking feedback from those who are younger and less experienced, they can use this knowledge to position their business to cater to the wants and needs of this more youthful audience. They become excited by being challenged on their conventional wisdom and are willing to look at things differently to find new ways to increase productivity and relevancy in the marketplace.

As a banker in Nashville, I have had the opportunity to work with professionals who write songs and own music publishing businesses. Many songwriters who have had a lot of highly profitable "hit" songs early in their careers may fade slowly into the background and you never hear from them again as they grow older.

However, I have seen a select few who took a completely different route. These older songwriters befriended some of the top new songwriters who were less than half their age. They hung out with them, got to know them, and wrote hit songs with them even into their old age. The interesting thing about these business owners is that through showing sincere interest in mentoring a new crop of young, "up-and-coming" songwriters in Nashville, they have been able to maintain relevance as songwriters in their own right. These business owners learned that networking with others who are different and younger can pay huge dividends.

As I mentioned about reaping what one sows, these owners also found that it was impossible not to benefit in a huge way themselves and in their business from helping others.

Here's the bottom line: *You can't get there by yourself and you certainly can't stay there by yourself.* It is imperative to develop a consistent habit of reaching out to others and building long-lasting relationships to truly achieve the maximum possible success with your business. If you isolate yourself, you also isolate your business. If you want your business to feed you and your family for a lifetime, make it a point to constantly feed your pipeline of contacts, centers of influence, and prospects. Not only will you grow your business, you will obtain the satisfaction that comes from connecting with others in such a way as to build a better community and a better life for all.

CHAPTER 5:

CHAPTER CHALLENGE

1. Consider all of the organizations in your area (Chamber of Commerce, Rotary Club, nonprofits, faith-based organizations, hobby or craft organizations, political organizations, and so forth). Identify two that you want to "sink your teeth into" over the next two years. My recommendation is that you spend time meeting all of the members. Go to lunch with many of them, serve on committees, and work side-by-side with other members to fulfill the work of the organization, and perhaps even serve as an officer for the organization.

2. Next, list all the people you know who might be able to help you with your business. This includes people who are "movers and shakers" in your community who should know the services or products you provide or will be providing. Leave no stone unturned as you think about all of the family, friends, neighbors, church members, and so forth with whom you have built relationships through your life. Just be sure that when you approach these people, the interaction is not one-sided. Don't go to these people simply asking for something. You may appear to be a "user" if you haven't talked to them in five or ten years, then call to ask

them to help you with business referrals or to per-sonally use the services of your business.

Instead, go to the people with a win-win propo-sition. Learn about their business, their profes-sion, and their needs and desires as you talk with them. Think of ways you can be of benefit to them. A win-win referral relationship goes a lot further and longer than one in which you are perceived as the "needy" person who asks them to give to you. You are too strong for that, so act like it. Every time you ask someone to use their contacts, skills, and so forth to help you or your business, you should ask yourself how you can do the same for them, unless you are paying them for their assistance.

3. Keep this contact list and each person's informa-tion and continue to add to it, as long as you own your business. Your list of contacts always should be up-to-date; you should type in new contacts to your phone and synchronize them with your com-puter on at least a weekly or monthly basis. These connections can be the lifeblood of your business. Make this a priority and always remember to give back so that you are welcomed on your next visit and not avoided. In doing so, you not only get help with accomplishing your goals and meeting your needs, you do the same for the other person. This can give you a feeling of accomplishment at a whole new level. Also, some of these people will become great friends and will be there to help you

when the toughest challenges come to your business in the future.

CHAPTER 6:

CASH IS KING

S tay high on cash and low on debt. The best time to build cash for your upcoming business venture is while you are working your "day job," looking forward to owning your own business, and designing your business plan. Cash is king in any business, and liquidity is your ability to easily and quickly convert assets to cash. Therefore, without an adequate amount of liquidity, no one should venture into starting up a business. Just because you write a well thought-out business plan does not mean that everything will go as planned. It doesn't mean you won't hit bumps in the road, or have unexpected challenges and costly delays. These types of issues are natural occurrences in the day-to-day life of a business owner. Cash, or liquidity, is the answer to all of these problems.

It may take six to twelve months for your initial sales plan to start to become a reality. If you don't have enough initial cash to sustain your business, pay your rent, compensate your employees, and fund your advertising, your business can come to a quick halt.

If there is not enough revenue to create a substantial profit, then your business will have to rely on either borrowing funds or using stored cash to continue to function in the lean times. This is when a storehouse of cash, saved when you worked for someone else and lived very modestly, becomes invaluable. You only want to take on debt in modest amounts over time for the sole purpose of enabling your business to grow (not to keep your business from closing because this is your only source of funding). The less debt you build on your business the better; avoiding debt is paramount. Remember, debt gives you funding for a period of time, but it has to be paid back—with interest. Too much debt, or leverage, can drain cash flow and cause your business to be insolvent.

A delicate balance of *debt* (borrowed funds) and *equity* (your ownership in your business) must be established and maintained throughout every life cycle of a business. If you go into a business without enough of your own capital (assets), then you will be forced to overborrow from the bank or other investors to get your business off the ground. A large debt load puts extreme pressure on both your business and yourself. It is also one of the best ways to lead to the rapid deterioration and even failure of your business before it really gets started.

Building cash on the front end is not exciting, sexy, or fun. It takes a lot of hard work and discipline, and is not glamorous at the time. However, for a business owner, building cash normally provides a whole lot more fun and success in the long-term. "Get rich quick" schemes don't work. An undisciplined business (or business owner) does not become highly successful. Even if the business grows quickly, decline can occur at just as rapid of a pace. Building habits of discipline before you build your business, will have immense pay-offs for you and your business down the road.

Living on 80 percent or less of your personal income is a habit that I encourage you to build for a lifetime. You need to develop a cushion or margin between what you make and what you spend. If you can spend 80 percent or less of your net income or take-home pay (after taxes), give 10 percent, and save 10 percent, you always should have enough. In addition, you will enjoy the blessing of being able to give to others who are less fortunate while also building up enough savings over time to cover you when unexpected expenses arise. The key to living on that 80 percent is that you have to be sure that your lifestyle is in line with your income. It takes discipline to keep your lifestyle from outpacing your income, no matter how much money you make.

Since it takes a lot of discipline to cut back and save cash before you start your business, most people don't perform this task adequately. That's why owners who do will reap enormous benefits and will be "head and shoulders" above the rest. Starting or running a business that is adequately funded provides a lot of advantages: better and more desirably priced lending options; the ability to better survive downturns in a particular industry or the overall economy; and the ability to stay calm when other businesses in your industry feel immense pressure due to the compression of high leverage and decreased sales.

You may ask: *How much cash is enough and how much debt is too much?* Well, it depends. If you go into detailed financial analysis, there are liquidity ratios, debt service coverage ratios, and debt-to-net worth ratios, which have acceptable ranges for businesses in various industries. However, from an overall perspective, the more cash you have and the less debt you have, the better.

As a general rule of thumb, it would be wise to have at least enough cash saved to cover six months of operating expenses before you start a new business. For a start-up business, I would recommend beginning with zero debt, if possible, because you have no track record to demonstrate that you can pay back debt. This initial term is challenging enough to simply get your revenues going so that you can begin to launch the business off the ground. Also, it may make sense to lease your space and equipment for an initial period. Not to be negative, but short-term leases are easier to get out of than long-term debt, if things go south.

When your business has proven to be a sustainable entity, taking on a reasonable amount of debt for the right reasons can be a wise move. Often, it can be a wise investment to purchase or build a commercial building to house your business. Also, it may be necessary to finance some of your equipment and company vehicles to keep up with demand for your products or services. Give enough time (at least a couple of years) to prove to yourself and the bank that you have a profitable and sustainable business before taking on debt, especially long-term debt like a building purchase.

When you decide to finance a building, equipment, or vehicles, I recommend putting down in cash at least 20 percent of the purchase price. If you can afford to put even more, do it. As a business owner, you always want to have as much cushion as possible between what you owe on an investment related to your business and what that asset is worth. Having equity (ownership value above what is owed on an asset) in all of the assets of your business gives you security and options in a financial downturn or economic crisis. Besides, it doesn't make financial sense to pay more interest on loans than you have to; put down as much as possible and borrow the least amount possible.

You should never borrow enough to strain your overall business cash flow. Your cash flow for any loan you take out on your business, combined with any existing debt you may have, should always yield at least a 1.25 percent debt service coverage ratio or higher. The debt service coverage ratio for your business is determined by dividing your annual net operating income (net profit) by the total amount of annual debt payments. A global debt service coverage ratio also includes your personal debt and your personal income in the mix.

If you are a small business owner and you own the majority of your business, and therefore benefit from receiving the majority of the business's profit, the global debt service coverage ratio is the best one to use. Having a minimum of a 1.25 percent debt service coverage ratio keeps you in an acceptable range, not only when borrowing for the business, but also to ensure that your personal lifestyle stays properly in line with your income. A 1.25 percent global debt service coverage ratio or higher means that for every dollar of debt service that you have related to your business and your personal life, you have at least $1.25 of after-tax income to support it. If you think about it as a ratio, a 1.25 percent global debt service coverage ensures that you always have at least a 25 percent cushion of cash flow over your cost of debt, and this is a good thing.

Another factor to consider when borrowing money is to keep enough liquidity (cash reserves, prefer-ably) to service the debt and other obligations for an extended period of time. Liquidity will help if you experience an economic downturn or a deterioration in sales. It ensures that you can take advantage of available opportunities when other businesses in your industry may be choking because they have run out of an adequate amount of cash flow. Difficult economic times will come, so being properly prepared enables your business to survive (and even thrive) while your competitors may be losing market share.

I advise my clients to keep at least 20 percent in personal liquidity of the amount they borrow. In simple math, if an experienced business owner wants to purchase a new building for $1,000,000 to house their business, they should consider putting down $200,000 in cash (20 percent of the sales price) and having another $160,000 in cash reserves (20 percent of the $800,000 they borrowed from the bank to com-plete the purchase of the building). This 20 percent of cash reserves not only can be used to service debt if the cash flow of the business is reduced, but it also can be used for normal and unexpected repairs and maintenance of the building.

If you are starting a new business, this amount of cash may seem overwhelming. However, don't let it deter you from planning to put away cash, no matter what stage your current business may be in. As I mentioned earlier, saying no to instant benefits from the profit of your business to build the discipline of storing up cash for a rainy day is a non-glamorous, difficult, and arduous process in the beginning. The amount of security and peace it will give you in the long run cannot be overestimated.

Building this type of discipline requires you to swim upstream compared to what the majority of business owners do. But down the road, it will pay off exponentially and will give you a strength that you will find no other way. Just like "time in the gym" sometimes doesn't show for the athlete until they are in the championship game, building a wealth of liquidity may not show until an economic or industry downturn puts the squeeze on your business.

It is true that a "borrower is a slave to the lender" (Proverbs 22:7, CSB). The more cash you save on the front end and the less debt you accumulate as your business grows, the better position you will be in. You will be able to maneuver through challenging times and also take advantage of unforeseen opportunities. Think of high liquidity and low debt as being critical to the overall health of your business. It is similar to how regular exercise and healthy eating are of benefit to your body. This kind of business protocol keeps a company healthy and makes it fit to weather challenging conditions, much like how a healthy body helps to ward off disease and sickness.

Another note regarding business debt: A line of credit is a useful tool for many mature businesses. As a business continues to grow, it may be impossible to have enough cash on hand to keep up with temporary fluctuations in inventory, paying vendors (accounts payable), and other seasonal or temporary demands. For this reason, a line of credit with a reasonable limit can be very helpful. A commercial line of credit has an established limit, and is like a huge credit card that can be drawn up and paid down at will. The good thing about this type of debt instrument is that you only pay interest on the amount of the line you use.

One important fact to know is that a line of credit only should be used to pay for temporary needs of the business. The business or commercial line of credit is never meant to be a long-term or permanent injection of capital. It should be drawn up to meet a specific need, then quickly paid back down once the business realizes profit from that investment. For instance, a line of credit may be utilized for seasonal needs. This could make sense for a retail business that has a high volume of sales for Christmas in November and December, then slows dramatically in January and February. Since customers may have spent a lot during the holiday season, the line of credit could be used for temporary payroll needs and restocking inventory in January and February when sales are slow. The loan then can be quickly paid down as sales and profits increase in March and April with new spring promotions.

Also, a line of credit could be used to pay manufacturers and suppliers quickly to obtain prompt payment discounts; then the loan should be paid down as soon as that inventory is sold and payment is received. A line of credit that doesn't fluctuate up and down frequently is not being used as a line of credit. If a line of credit is drawn up and stays at a high level for an extended period of time, it is really an "evergreen" line and is acting as a permanent capital infusion into the business. If this is the case, the line should be converted to a fixed term and fixed interest rate loan, and extinguished as quickly as possible through regular principal and interest payments.

An "evergreen" line of credit is often a warning sign that the business is not profitable enough on its own to meet all of its financial obligations. Therefore, a business owner will be wise only to use on a line of credit an amount that can be paid back in a fairly brief period of time through a progression of the sales cycle.

There is a reason why I have written an entire chapter on how important liquidity is and how dangerous debt can be. These are two components, that when not balanced carefully, have taken down more good businesses than anything else I have witnessed. A business owner can bypass the discipline of saving and building liquidity and move quickly into debt, getting "over their head" before they realize it.

The sad truth is that I have seen business owners get into debt early in their business and pay for it for a decade or more (and sometimes never recover). Debt is not something to be taken lightly; you should be sure that any decision to take on debt is made only after consulting with professionals you trust (your C.P.A., banker, attorney, and fellow business owners). Most financial decisions should be made slowly and cautiously after much thought and counsel. It is easy to get into debt and so difficult to get out, so be sure that if you choose this route, it is a well thought-out process.

If you go into a business with a disciplined financial process that requires you to do the hard things on the front end and enjoy the benefits on the back end, you will always be ahead of the game. Taking the easy way by embracing debt early in a business may be satisfying at the time. But unfortunately, early debt often can have you paying a high price (not just in interest) for years and even can lead to the ultimate failure of your business.

Remember, I am a banker who makes his living by lending millions of dollars each year to profitable businesses to help them grow. If anyone understands the benefits of borrowing money for a business, I believe I would qualify. But I care enough about you long-term that I want to warn you to be careful in this area. My desire is for you to have a long lasting and profitable business that will sustain you, your family, and your employees for a lifetime. Take it from me: Fall in love with cash and liquidity, and always be cautious when it comes to borrowing money. I have no doubt that you will thank me for this bit of advice down the road.

CHAPTER 6:

CHAPTER CHALLENGE

1. Take time to assess where you are financially right now. Obtain a blank personal financial statement (locate one online or obtain one from a banker you know), then list all of your assets (valuable things you own) and liabilities (debts you owe). If you are already a business owner, print a current balance sheet for your business from QuickBooks. These two documents can provide invaluable insight into how you are doing in relation to storing cash and wisely using debt. Once you rate yourself on how you think you are doing, share these documents with your C.P.A. and a banker you trust, and ask for their honest assessment related to the industry you are in and the business you are building or planning to build.

2. Be prepared to make a plan of action according to what you learn from these assessments. For instance, if you are nowhere near where you need to be in terms of liquidity to start a business, don't be discouraged; let it motivate you. Let it provide the drive you need to build up the reserves necessary to survive long-term in a business when downturns come. Don't take the easy way out and ignore this crucial part of long-term success and staying power. Be willing to pay the price on the front end

after you get an honest evaluation of where you are in relation to where you should be.

If your business is already well under way, make a decision and a commitment to doing what it takes to put yourself in a stronger and more liquid position. When the hard times and unexpected challenges hit, you will be glad you did.

You may be over your head in personal debt, or your business may be highly leveraged. Consider it a gift that you see this for what it is while you still have a chance to do something about it. Start now to prepare yourself for a better tomorrow. If you have not yet launched your business, do yourself a favor and put everything on pause until you are in a stronger financial position. Never become impatient or impulsive when it comes to making financial decisions for yourself and your business.

The best way to ensure that you make wise financial decisions is not to become emotional with money matters. If you see that you do not have the staying power to hang in there long-term, then hold off launching your business until you are ready. You will be glad you did and you still will have plenty of time to make a go of it after you have paid the price to get yourself ready. Do the hard things first, then the rest of the journey will be easier. Otherwise, the fun you have starting a business may be your best days, and you could live to pay for it for many years to come if you go into it haphazardly and unprepared.

3. Be accountable to your C.P.A. and banker, and don't pull the trigger on launching your business until you are in a solid position. If your business is already moving forward, have the courage and the maturity to tap the brakes with growth until you are in a better and stronger position. You always can slow your growth while you build more liquidity and slow down the use of leverage. While it may be a tough pill to swallow in the near term, your future will be a lot brighter, and your business will be able to endure a lot more headwinds and unexpected challenges. Be willing to pay the price on the front end in order to enjoy the benefits afterward.

CHAPTER 7:

TALENT IS THE KEY TO UNLOCK THE FUTURE

As you plan the building of your business, don't forget the most important component: obtaining the best employees who will help improve your plan and best present your business to the public. Hopefully, in your years of working for someone else in the industry of your choice, you have identified and built relationships with some of the best and brightest who know your industry well. While this is no time to be intimidated, it is the best time to surround yourself with people who are smarter and more talented than you in multiple areas.

Your first hires are the most important as they will help to put an identity on your business, as well as to start the momentum. The time to begin having conversations with these initial employees is months and even years before you actually open your business. Determine any "pain" points they may have in their current job and see if you can design a new position for them that will remedy their pain, plus give them some "extras" that they get excited about (a more flexible schedule, a small ownership percentage, more authority, a better title, and so forth). Give these future employees of yours a dream for a better life and a more exciting and enjoyable job that they can think on while you put together the components of your business. They will enjoy being a part of the process and will tend to be more committed to you if they feel they are an important part of building this new entity.

Once you hire your first few employees and have built trust with them and in them, (hopefully a lot of this was done even prior to them coming to work for you), give them freedom and encouragement to offer suggestions to help you continually improve the plan. No business owner has all of the good ideas, so utilize to the fullest the creativity, intellect, and experience of your employees to help you to strive for continuous improvement and growth.

Businesses must innovate or die over time. Look at Taco Bell. They are a great example of a business that continuously modifies their product offering, then markets these product variations in such a way as to create renewed interest. If you think about it, Taco Bell has been selling the exact same ingredients for years: beef, cheese, and taco shells. They continually design new products with these same ingredients, put them into a different package, give them a new name, and market them as if they are revolutionary.

Throughout the years, this innovation and marketing strategy continues to work well for Taco Bell. Hiring top notch employees and utilizing their creative ideas can assist you as you innovate and improve on your original business plan in order to capture more market share in your industry.

Many of us like to surround ourselves with people who look, act, and think like we do. This can be disastrous when building a business. Establishing an overall culture and hiring people who fit well into that culture is important (characteristics of a business culture might entail such things as integrity, values, work ethic, striving for excellence, and rigorous customer service).

Equally important is to hire employees from different backgrounds with creative ideas and who possess a willingness to vocalize these ideas (in the proper way and with a respectful attitude). If you choose to hire most employees who are like you, then you will come up woefully short in covering all of the bases for your business. It is the melding of ideas, personalities, and skill sets that can make a business well-rounded, leading to a business that is highly profitable and successful in all areas.

For this reason, a business owner must be vulnerable and honest enough to discover what she or he does best and, just as important, what she or he is not good at. No matter how good or smart you think you are, the fact is that God didn't give anyone the ability to be good at everything or to not have blind spots. Getting a cross section of talent who are all working in the area of their primary giftedness will take a business to a whole other stratosphere.

If you haven't solidified in your mind yet what you are really good at and what you are not, conduct an anonymous 360-degree feedback program with your current employees and supervisors (provided, of course, that you are currently working for someone else). Also, solicit feedback from friends, customers, and family who know you best and who have been around you the most. You may be surprised at what you will find. A word of warning: accept their feedback gracefully, even if it hurts. A gold nugget of truth is usually present, even in the most critical or hurtful feedback, if you are willing to accept it. Accepting and embracing this feedback may well assist you in your growth as a leader more than anything else you do.

Remember, none of us are good at everything, but each of us is good at something. Find that something you're the best at and help your employees to find it too. Then allow them to adjust at least some of their job responsibilities to encompass their area or areas of strength. This exercise not only will enhance your overall business, it will create happier employees who are much more likely to stay employed at your business for a longer term. This, in turn, will create and sustain greater efficiencies in your business.

Loyal, happy, long-term employees can become your greatest asset and they also can keep the business running without your constant involvement over time, giving you more opportunity to enjoy the fruits of your labor. In the initial stages of your business, when your number of employees is small, it may become a very close-knit organization in which everyone feels like they are in a battle together, on the same team, and "having each other's backs" so that all areas are covered. The challenge is to keep this feeling among your employees as your company continues to grow.

Effective employee engagement is a key to keeping loyal workers. Conducting regular "brain-storming" sessions with all employees can give everyone the opportunity to voice what they think is working well, what needs to be changed, and offer ideas for affecting this change. It is important that no one's ideas or thoughts are shot down or criticized, as this will only kill creativity and employee engagement.

As your company grows and your number of employees increases, these brain-storming sessions may need to be conducted by various other company employees as well as yourself. Employees' opinions matter to them, and if you are a smart business owner, their opinions will matter to you also.

There is an old saying that goes like this: "Listen to the whispers and you won't have to hear the screams." I'm not sure who first said this, but they must have had a lot of wisdom. Give your employees a lot of opportunities to give their honest feedback to include what they would like to see changed and what they really don't like about their work environment or the company protocol. You will extinguish the embers that heat up, that can turn into flames, and eventually create fires that can cause inefficiency and block progress in your company.

Of course, you not only must give employees opportunities to voice concerns and suggestions for improvement, but you must actively listen to these comments and demonstrate that over time you are making positive changes from these suggestions. Employees should be able to see that at least a reasonable amount of their suggestions end up becoming reality in some form over time.

This does not mean that you don't have the final say and that some things you have designed and decided for your business are not absolutes. There will be some aspects about your business and your culture that you will need to hold to and not allow to change, no matter who doesn't like it. There definitely will be times when even some good employees are not a good fit for your business and your culture, and they will need to find a position elsewhere.

You need to decide early which "hills you will die on," and be sure that all of the lesser things about your business are up for discussion and for continual change and improvement. Even though you created the mold of the business on the potter's wheel, your best employees should have their fingerprints all over the mold before it hardens. Think more of what you can do together, and you will be a better team builder. You will end up having a more successful business than if you only use mainly your ideas and strengths.

Another important note about seeking employee feedback is that you must set clear guidelines for what is acceptable behavior in this process. Your employees should have guidance of the times, channels, and ways of expression that are acceptable and encouraged for this feedback. If employees know that they will have set times and channels to provide this feedback, it will give them security that their ideas will be heard, and also will allow you to maintain control over the ways that feedback is shared.

I have always told my employees that I am glad to listen to any feedback or suggestions they have for our bank or for me, as long as it is delivered in a professional and respectful manner. As an owner, you need to outline the details of what this means to you, and designate at which meetings and times that this is encouraged. Be sure to allow openings for suggestions for improvement and changes along with criticism of the process (as long as it is delivered in a professional and constructive way). These suggestions should be considered on some type of consistent basis so that you can know the issues and address them long before they become a major problem.

What a shame it would be to lose trusted employees, great customers, and future business because you were too busy to hear feedback from people working for you. They can save you from one or more dire mistakes if only you make the time to listen.

As a business owner, if you don't have a strong sense of self and a strong confidence in who you are and what you were put on earth to do, it would be good to work on developing these traits. Usually, and ironically, this is done through humility and not through arrogance as one might expect.

Realizing that you are only one person that God put here on this earth and that you don't have all of the answers helps you realize that you need others. It also helps you to truly appreciate the various gifts that others can bring. When you can acknowledge and celebrate the strengths of others because you are aware that it takes a team to build a highly successful business, you are well on your way to being a team builder for whom employees will go the extra mile in the marketplace.

You also must balance this attitude with confidence in yourself and your abilities. Appreciating who you are and what you bring to the table is a non-negotiable item. As the business owner, you must be the leader, self-starter, driver, cheerleader, rock, guide, and one who demonstrates unyielding commitment to the task and a never-give-up attitude. It is big shoes to fill, right? That's why owning your own business is both a joyous privilege and a huge responsibility that never goes away.

In your quest for hiring the best employees, look for people who love a challenge and who get a thrill out of continually making themselves and everything around them better and better. Those who seek continuous improvement are not going to be satisfied with the status quo. They always will seek ways to improve the process, increase the sales, innovate the product, increase the level of customer service, and so forth.

You want employees who are gutsy enough to take calculated risks and who believe in their hearts that if they make a mistake or fall short, they can recover and still will be better off for having had the courage to try. While you can teach and build certain characteristics in employees through your leadership, it is very difficult to take those who lack motivation and drive, and turn them into highly-productive assets to your company.

In addition, it is very difficult to create in an employee a work ethic and the internal accountability of one who believes in giving their best to what their hand finds to do. Be sure you look at potential employees' track records to know what they have done at school and in former job positions, and listen carefully to the words they use in interviews. Ask direct questions to others who have worked with them and for them, and who have managed them. Try to find people in your industry that you know and trust who have worked with them and who do not appear on their reference list. These people can tell you the truth about the person you are looking to bring on board, and can save you future heartache and time. They can let you know if you are about to hire someone who may end up being a drain to you and your business.

As the old saying goes, "be slow to hire and quick to fire." While I don't encourage terminating anyone's employment without giving them plenty of opportunities to make improvements, if you realize you made a bad decision with a hire, take action quickly to remedy the issue. Don't allow yourself to avoid these difficult tasks or it will cripple your business. It also will discourage your good and great employees if you allow someone to continue working long-term who is either incapable or unwilling to make the changes needed to produce work at an acceptable or exceptional level.

Additionally, retaining employees who deliver unacceptable performance is unfair to the employees themselves. While they may not like it at the time, if they are not the right fit for their current job, your helping them see this will eventually give them the opportunity to find something that is a better fit long-term. If they have character or work ethic issues, they need to see this clearly as well so that they know the truth and can make choices to change this in their next position, if they choose to do so.

Don't make the mistake of thinking that because someone is more skilled than you in certain areas, more educated than you, or perhaps more intelligent than you that this person does not need to be working for you. By all means, hire them and let them shine in your company. This makes you and your company look better. After all, a championship hockey coach is not expected to be able to out-skate or outshoot every player on the team. But if he or she can get the right people on the team in the appropriate roles, give them the guidance they need to be successful, and let them shine doing what they do best, who cares if they can even skate at all. Get the picture? Just do what you do best and assemble the best team possible. Always look for that next addition to your team that can help to take you to the next level.

A final word of guidance on this topic: As a business owner, you need to become a recruiter who is constantly on the lookout for your next hire, until you have someone who is top notch at doing this for you. Even then, keep this skill sharpened because you never know when you will need it again.

Over the last 15 years, I have made a practice of taking a couple of bankers to lunch each month, simply to build a deeper relationship with them and a larger sense of trust between us. Even if they are happy where they are at the time, I want to build a strong enough relationship that I am their first phone call if they ever consider making a change.

You will find that this is time and effort well spent because some of your best hires over time will be the result of years, not months, of relationship building and vision casting. As a business owner, you only will be as successful as the quality of employees and partners that you can bring on your team. Therefore, consider one of your chief jobs to be that of a recruiter, at least for the first few years, and possibly for the entire life of the business.

Going after the best of the best and keeping them motivated and engaged is not for those who don't like a challenge. But isn't that part of the reason you became a business owner in the first place, because you love a challenge and you like to have a part in controlling your own destiny? Don't shrink back from taking on the competition in your industry to find, hire, coach up and mentor, and retain the best of the best for your company. They are the lifeblood of your business, so be sure you take great care of them and let them shine.

CHAPTER 7:

CHAPTER CHALLENGE

1. Make a list of the top 10 employees that you would
    recruit today if money and their willingness to
    move was not an obstacle. Then reach out to them
    one by one to schedule a lunch date with them.
    Find out what makes them tick and what they may
    be looking for that they don't have in their current
    position. If you see that there is no way to con-
    vince them to move to your company right now, ask
    about acquaintances who may be as good as they
    are who might be in a different position and ask for
    an introduction. Also, remember to keep these top
    guns on your rotation list so that you get together
    for lunch with each of them at least once every
    six months to keep in touch and build trust, just in
    case anything changes with their current situations.
    I always tell potential recruits that even if they have
    no interest in moving currently, I would like to earn
    the right to be their first phone call if something
    changes with their status or contentment level.

    Don't make recruiting a one-time task. Keep a
    revolving list to go through each month, year in and
    year out. Even if you are fully staffed, you always
    need to be looking for additional bench strength
    should something change with your business or
    should one of your employees unexpectedly decide

to change companies, move to another state, or potentially change careers. Always be prepared for employee turnover in your business, as it will happen, and often it will come at the most inconvenient times. Do not lie back and wait for something to happen that could leave you flat-footed. You need to be proactive and always be on the hunt for your next high performing employee who could fill a vacancy or who could add to an already productive team to help take your company to another level.

2. If you already own your own company, when was the last time that you asked for suggestions and gave each employee a chance to let you know their biggest frustrations and pain points of working at your business? When was the last time when you solicited feedback that was hard to hear? When was the last time when you prodded, encouraged, and drew out critical comments from your employees to see what their real challenges were?

    If your answer to the previous questions is "never," "years ago," or even "months ago," you have work to do. Remember the advice of "listen to the whispers and you will not have to hear the screams." If you don't regularly ask to hear the whispers, you are setting yourself up to think everything is going great, then out of nowhere you may hear some screams that shock you. Don't assume that everything is going great and that everyone is happy working at your company just because you don't hear them complaining.

You may have a lot happier employees if they feel comfortable enough to complain some around you. This shows that they believe their opinion is valued and they trust you enough to not simply tell you what they think you want to hear. Human nature is such that people who work for you are not going to look on the bright side all of the time. Give them the ability to share these negative thoughts and feelings, and you will diminish their effect on your employees and on your business. Remember to sincerely listen and make appropriate changes when an employee has a good point. Look at it as free, in-house consulting. You received a suggestion that could improve your business and you didn't have to pay extra for it past what you already have in salary expense.

3. Be sure to give your employees regular opportunities to challenge the status quo, to disagree with some company initiatives, and to contribute to making the process better for all. Employees will sometimes feel overlooked, ignored, unimportant, and unappreciated, no matter how good of a leader you may be. Give them the chance to say so and to share with you what it will take to make things better. It takes a lot of humility and a lot of courage from you to do this, but it will make a night-and-day difference in the long-term viability and quality of

your company. It also will help you develop a fertile ground for recruiting top talent.

You will find that your employees will become your best advocates to others in your industry when they share with them how much they enjoy working for your company. Remember: Most employees don't leave a job because of their company, but because of their manager or the company's leadership.

CHAPTER 8:

ACCOUNTABILITY PARTNERS

Accountability is a tough word that is only useful to people who want to be their best and do their best. Accountability is often painful. It's like pruning a tree so it can grow to its fullest, most beautiful potential. To reach your personal full potential, as well as the full potential of your business, you must develop a set of professional accountability partners. You should meet with these accountability partners on a regular basis, at least quarterly, if not monthly. Give them complete permission to tell you what you need to hear, not just what you want to hear.

My suggestion is that you find a C.P.A., a banker, an attorney, and an investment advisor as your professional accountability partners, as well as a couple of high-integrity friends as your personal accountability partners. This sets you up for a good business and personal life, which often become intertwined and mutually dependent when you own your own business. Any big mistakes you make in your business can drastically affect your personal life (your income, the hours you are required to work, your stress level). Likewise, any big mistake that you make in your personal life can drastically affect your business (living an extravagant lifestyle, having an affair, not taking good care of your body, and so forth).

Accountability partners in your personal and professional life can serve as guardrails to keep you on the road and to keep you from veering off track. While I'll leave it up to you to find two friends who can hold you accountable in your personal life, I will share advice on why and how the professional accountability partners can add value.

Let's start by discussing the function and benefit of having a trusted Certified Public Accountant. A C.P.A. who has years of experience working with businesses has usually walked through every stage of a business cycle from origination to sale or closure. They have expert advice on the tax consequences of every move you make in your business. They can advise you as to how to best set up your business (as an LLC, S Corp, C Corp, Partnership, and so forth) to attempt to accomplish the desired tax advantages. They can advise you regularly on what tax advantages are available with every move and stage of your business (e.g.–when using a Section 179 deduction for equipment purchases is appropriate).

I advise getting C.P.A. referrals from other business owners or from commercial bankers who know their reputation. It is wise to meet with at least three C.P.A.s initially to determine their level of experience with businesses similar to yours, their cost, and their personality and service level. Take your time to find that person with whom you can work day-in and day-out over the long-term. This person can be a huge asset, or liability, to your business, so you must choose wisely.

Once you find and retain your C.P.A.'s services, be sure to talk with her or him about every major financial decision related to your business *before* you make that decision. Your C.P.A. can help you a lot more on the front end, than when trying to assist in cleaning up on the back end after a poor financial decision has been made.

Next, find a trusted and experienced business attorney who also can come from referrals of a commercial banker or your new C.P.A. The attorney needs to have a depth of experience with setting up legal entities, along with a background in business litigation and employment law, and an expertise in contract review and negotiation.

Your attorney can work with your C.P.A. to ensure that the way you set up your business not only gives you the maximum possible tax advantages, but also gives you maximum legal protection. Your attorney can assist with helping you set up internal employee policy guidelines and procedures that can help you avoid potential lawsuits and other obstacles down the road. You will undoubtedly become involved with leases and other contracts that will need a legal review prior to execution, so continual engagement with your attorney will be necessary.

In addition, it will not be unusual for you or your business to be listed in one or multiple lawsuits throughout the tenure of your business, no matter how careful you may be. Your attorney can help you to avoid many lawsuits through her or his counsel, while already being familiar with your business and ready to assist when an unfortunate lawsuit does occur.

My next suggestion is my favorite one for obvious reasons. Find a trusted business and commercial banker who often can be located through referrals from your C.P.A. or attorney. An experienced and well-educated commercial banker has seen the financials of dozens, and maybe even hundreds, of businesses like yours. This person should be familiar with your particular industry and should be able to offer a lot of wisdom that can assist you through the growth of your business. A strong commercial banker has watched many businesses grow with a bird's eye view of their financials and should have much to offer in wise counsel that can help you take advantage of opportunities, while also avoiding pitfalls that other businesses have fallen into.

A banker is limited legally on the extent in which they can advise you on your business decisions (so that they won't be considered accountable for your decisions). However, they are allowed to share what they have seen and what they have learned in generic fashion (without giving confidential details about the business or businesses they learned from). Their experience can be incredibly valuable to you in helping you to ascertain when to step on the gas and when to tap the brakes.

A good commercial banker also can help you with balancing debt and growth along with helping you to take full advantage of your cash flow. (They can use tools such as Treasury Management services to assist in collecting cash as quickly as possible from sales, then managing that cash as efficiently as possible).

A great commercial banker will offer a lot more than the lowest rate on a loan or the highest rate on a deposit account. In fact, a business owner would be wise not to let the decision of who they bank with be determined solely by pricing. Experience, expertise, service, and concern for you and your business can be a lot more important from a long-term perspective when deciding on who your primary banker will be.

Once you have your C.P.A., attorney, and banker chosen, it is wise to introduce the three of them (if they are not already familiar with each other) and encourage collaboration between you and all three of these professionals. The best decisions for your business will be made when the perspectives of all three of these professionals are considered along with your own. Many mistakes can be avoided when you invite advice from all of these team members. This gives you a holistic perspective that can help your business maintain the balance that will achieve maximum success.

It is actually a great idea to have quarterly and "specially-called" meetings with your C.P.A., your attorney, and your banker all in the same room at the same time. This way everyone gets to hear how a decision involving your business will create impact in all directions. This time set aside and the compensation costs for these professionals is a small price to pay for the benefits you will receive.

A financial advisor is also important to help you make wise plans and investments with the money you make from the profit of your business. All of your financial livelihood is normally tied to your business, so it is important that you pay yourself well. Pay yourself for the work you put in and the risks you take (as long as it is not so well that you pay yourself unreasonably to the detriment of your business) and properly invest every hard-earned dollar you make. Even in the early years when you are planning for the start of your business, your investment advisor can help you to maximize your gain from the money you are putting back while keeping you well-positioned in safe, liquid investments.

An investment advisor is equally important even in the initial lean years of beginning your business. She or he can help you properly invest whatever you make and can assist you in continuing to develop the discipline of saving and investing. This will become immensely important as you approach the time of retirement. It is not wise to plan your whole retirement on simply the "one-day" sale of your business. It is much wiser to put away money little by little, like the ant, and watch it grow through smart, conservative investments.

There is no guarantee that you will find a ready buyer for your business; and there is certainly no guarantee that you will be able to command the price you have in mind for the sale of your business when the time comes for you to step back from it. If the "one day" sale of your business makes you filthy rich, then good for you! But why not save and invest wisely along the way so that you can have financial peace of mind, no matter what happens at the expiration of your work life?

A financial advisor who is experienced at working with business owners can help you not only to plan for your own retirement, but also for the retirement of your loyal, long-term employees. In addition to perhaps setting up a SEP (Simplified Employed Pension) plan for you as the owner, the financial advisor can assist you with setting up a proper retirement vehicle for the employees of your company, such as a 401K or ESOP (Employee Stock Ownership Plan). This can go a long way in creating loyalty from your best employees when they see that you are equally interested in insuring that they too are well taken care of for the long-term.

As discussed in the previous chapter, no one is good at everything, and as a business owner, you will have many blind spots. You often will be so busy and so pulled with the day-to-day operations and decision making for your business that you will have little time to think of anything else. This is why it is imperative to have tenured professionals in various disciplines who are watching all of the major financial and legal areas of your business for potential pitfalls and to ensure that you are taking advantage of opportunities to the full extent.

Think of you and your employees as the fort that contains the heart of the business, and your outside advisors as the moat surrounding the fort to protect it from unnecessary attacks. These professionals will be well worth the money spent if you listen to them and take their advice seriously. While you don't always have to go with every piece of their advice, you are foolish if you completely ignore their warnings or stern suggestions. Let them help you and embrace them as an important part of the team. I don't think you will ever be sorry for doing this.

With choosing good financial and legal account-ability partners, you will be well on your way to achieving the proper balance on tough decisions after assessing the risks and rewards. You will be able to find that middle-of-the-road between doing it "your way" and taking the advice of others who "have your back." Even though it is still your team and it is still your busi-ness, this additional guidance will pay huge dividends over the course of your time in business.

I am always impressed when a new client tells me that they would like for me to meet their C.P.A. and their attorney. I know this is a client whom I can assist with their banking needs right off the bat in most every circumstance. Why? Because I know that if they have already been seeking the financial and legal advice of a C.P.A. and an attorney, then they should have made enough wise decisions to keep them out of financial and legal trouble; and they should be in a pretty good financial position, both personally and business wise.

Another thing I know about this future client is that she or he is wise enough to listen to experts who can assist them in growing their business and making it more profitable. I usually choose not to work with "know-it-alls" who think that my services are simply a commodity. I much prefer to spend my time, especially at this point in my career, helping people who are wise enough to value the expertise that everyone brings to the table. It is also a true pleasure to see these types of business owners reap the success of their wisdom and humility as the years go by.

I have an example that I would like to share. I was introduced to a C.P.A. in Franklin, Tennessee, which is located in Williamson County, the most affluent county in Tennessee. This C.P.A. was in his 50s at the time and was one of the most sought after C.P.A.s in the area as he had tremendous wisdom, expertise, and experience in working with many top business owners throughout Middle Tennessee. I was referred to this C.P.A. by one of his customers, and we were introduced and worked together with many mutual clients over the years.

This C.P.A. was adamant that any new client he referred to me was to be introduced while we were all three together and could have a conversation about building cohesion for the good of that business owner. We all would usually go out to lunch together on a periodic basis after the initial introduction, then spend time together at the actual business with the owner from time to time.

This highly-skilled C.P.A. understood that I as the banker had to know continually what was going on with the business, while he also knew that he needed to be aware of everything I was doing for this client on the banking side. It was a really good partnership of professionals as we worked together and cared deeply about the success of the businesses that we were sup-porting. We also grew to be good friends over time and had fun celebrating the triumphs of each business that we worked with through the years.

I found out why this C.P.A. was so successful, why he was highly sought after, and why he charged a very high per-hour rate that his clients didn't mind paying. This C.P.A. made sure that all of the bases were covered and that all of the professionals supporting this business stayed in touch and were well aware of all of the moving parts. This full disclosure paid off handsomely for the business owner and the success of her or his business. I noticed that it also gave the business owner tremendous confidence in their decision making regarding the business. The business owner knew that he or she had a full range of wisdom behind every decision made, which came from some very competent experts.

You need to be strong in your opinion and in your leadership of the company; be sure to make the decisions that you really feel are the right ones for the company. However, I advise you to always balance your intuition and your "gut" with sound advice from the professionals who have spent their career learning the details of transactions that can help or harm your business. The right kind of leader and business owner is strong enough to listen to those who can help him or her to guide the ship in the best direction and at the best speed, and to choose the right time to move forward with certain initiatives in order to realize maximum profitability and balanced growth.

We talked earlier about how important recruiting the best employees is to the proper growth of your business. This same effort is needed as well in being sure you recruit the best financial and legal professionals to your team. Don't be in a rush, but do be intentional with this recruiting. This team needs to be built early on. In addition to considering their expertise, reputation, and experience, be sure that each member is someone who shares your overall values and whom you would enjoy spending time with frequently. If you end up hiring them to be one of your advisors, you will spend an incredible amount of time with them over the next several years.

The bottom line: even though you are the business owner and ultimately what you say goes, you are wise to listen closely to the advice of a few professional experts who can protect your blind spots. If you don't have the humility and the wisdom to do this, you may find yourself sacrificing the great idea you had for a business due to a technicality that could have been avoided. The trouble is, by that point you may have wasted your life savings only to have to start all over working for someone else. Don't be that person. Be the wise business owner who built his business on the rock, not on the sand. Seek out and listen to wise counsel from those who make it their profession.

CHAPTER 8:

CHAPTER CHALLENGE

1. Do you have a trusted C.P.A., attorney, banker, and financial advisor? If not, start with the C.P.A., then move to the attorney, the banker, and the financial advisor, if you already own your own business or are starting up your business. If you are still in the planning stage of launching your business, start out with securing a good personal financial advisor. Like the airline steward or stewardess who tells you first to put on your air mask in the event of a loss of cabin pressure so that you still will be around to help others put on their air mask, you must be sure that you are strong financially before launching your own business that will employ and support others.

   Always go on recommendations from people you know and trust who have utilized the services of one of these professionals themselves for several years. Also, you can take recommendations from professionals you know and trust who have clients who have successfully used one of these professionals for several years and who know their reputation.

   Since you probably have a personal checking account at a bank, you always can receive free advice and recommendations on a C.P.A. and attorney from a business or commercial banker who works at your bank. Your bank also may have a good recommendation for an investment advisor, as most banks now employ an investment and insurance department within their bank holding company. However, don't go to this person just because they are with your bank. Interview a couple of other investment advisors who are with another bank or a separate investment firm to compare their experience, credentials, and their ability to offer investments outside of a particular portfolio offering. Also, be sure that she or he has a personality and respect for risk that fits well with your own.

2. I would suggest that you interview at least three professionals in each of the categories of C.P.A., banker, attorney, and investment advisor. Don't be afraid also to ask the one you feel the best about for three or more references of clients, other professionals, and so forth, whom you can call to ask questions about the quality and trustworthiness of their work. These professionals will have a huge impact on your personal financial position and the success and longevity of your business. Therefore, it is very important to take your time in order to select the best fit for you and your business in each of these positions.

3. Give yourself a time limit for selecting these individual professionals and put the end date on your calendar so that you don't forget and you are

held accountable for getting this task completed. I would suggest giving yourself two or three months, if needed, and not more than six months maximum. Also, be sure these individuals are willing to work with the other members of your team. It might be a worthwhile exercise to have all of these individuals to meet together with you for lunch when you think you have selected the right players for your team. I would suggest having this meeting before you make your final selections to ensure that these various personalities can "gel" together and work alongside each other for your good and the collective good of your business.

Also, if you ask these individuals to lunch while you are still in the selection process, they all would probably agree not to bill you for their time (the C.P.A. and attorney usually charge by the hour or appointment) since they are still being interviewed for a potential long-term position of working with your company. For the cost of everyone's lunch, you will get a bird's eye view of just how willing they are to work together and how interactive and accepting of each other's expertise they will be.

Take your time with this exercise, but don't take too long. Be sure these individuals are selected and engaged, then be sure you take their advice into consideration on a regular basis. While you may choose to override their advice at certain critical junctures of your business growth, be wise enough to thoroughly consider their advice so that you go into every situation with your eyes wide open.

CHAPTER 9:

THE ULTIMATE SUPPORT GROUP

You have probably noticed that even if you are a 100 percent owner of your business, I don't recommend going it alone or existing in a vacuum. There's too much growing and learning to be gained from others, including your employees, your financial and legal professionals, and your fellow business owners. When it comes to your association with other business owners, there are three simple categories to consider: those less experienced than you, the ones with a similar amount of experience and success as you, and those who have a lot more experience and have achieved a great deal more success than you.

Let's start by discussing why you want to spend some of your time each year with another business owner who has less experience than you. The mentoring and teaching that you do for this person not only will help them immensely, it also will help you to clarify why you do what you do; it will enable you to get even better through teaching. This activity also will help keep you enthused about your business as you are reminded of how much you've learned and how far you've come. You always win by giving back. You may not be at a point yet in which you can mentor anyone who is running a business. Even so, I'm sure someone took time with you to teach you some of what they've learned about starting and running a company.

When you get to the point in which you have some experience, wisdom, and knowledge to offer someone else, be sure to do it, for them and for you. Who knows, one day you may end up writing a book about all you've learned from running your own business! It could help those who are just starting out or those who are not as far along in the process as you are at the time.

Another benefit of mentoring and teaching a less experienced or "want to be" business owner is that it helps you to remember all that you've accomplished so far on your journey. It is very fulfilling when you realize that where you are right now is where a lot of others eventually want to get. It helps you to appreciate and be thankful for all you've learned and the level of success that God has blessed you with to date. We all have a tendency to take our lives for granted, and to forget how far we've come and how blessed we are. Taking time to give advice and teach another who is not as far down the road reminds us how good we've got it and how much our hard work has paid off.

Next, let's talk about those fellow business owners who are your peers and who have an equivalent amount of experience compared to you. Whereas mentoring may be better as a one-on-one activity conducted a few times per year, development through meeting with peer business owners is often beneficial when done in a group. You will often discover a lot of synergy, camaraderie, and encouragement from these peer relationships.

Even though those of you in the group may be similar in regard to your amount of experience with running a business and with the level of success you have achieved to date, you each will have learned different things along the way and will have different strengths. Because of this, group discussions about challenges you have in your business can open up a flood of ideas and strategies that you may never have considered. Just having a group of trusted peers (this trust, of course, will take time to build) that you can share your struggles and your triumphs with will be freeing and motivating for you. When it comes to obstacles and challenges in a business, being able to open up about these things with peers who won't judge or criticize you can be extremely uplifting. There is a real payoff when you add in the feedback of this group, offering suggestions for how you can overcome these challenges.

Being a business owner can be one of the loneliest jobs anywhere, because you are separated from your employees through your ownership and your position. You also are separated from your customers because you are there to please them and to make a profit from their use of your products or services.

Gathering with other business owners who are exposed to some of the same areas of isolation that you are can give all of you some camaraderie and take away some of the loneliness that often comes with the position. In a funny way, you can look at it as if putting a lot of misfits in a room together, and suddenly they are no longer misfits. Because they have so much in common, they can relate to each other's challenges and strengths, and soon they become like a family. Because everyone has similar challenges and struggles as a business owner, you can build cohesiveness rather quickly.

Another benefit of having this type of peer group is that, unless you are direct competitors in a particular industry, you won't have to worry about being transparent and opening up about your weaknesses, struggles, or any discouragements that come along. Of course, as I mentioned earlier, building a small group that you can trust with your weaknesses and struggles will definitely take some time. I would never encourage you to walk into a group and throw out your greatest struggles until you get to a level of trust with the individuals in that group that only comes with time. Even if it takes several years, just think of how much you all can grow together through sharing ideas and think about how much this group can help you through the changing seasons of your business.

Many CEO and business-owner peer groups exist. Some are specific to certain industries, some are exclusively for women or minorities, and some are more general in nature. Find or start one that is right for you and allow yourself to grow with these other individuals who have many of the same goals and dreams as you. I suggest a once a month meeting over lunch or dinner to keep you all engaged and building the cohesiveness in your group that will enable you to trust and encourage each other. Ten to twelve members is a good number as long as people are highly committed to this group and willing to make the sacrifices necessary to attend at least 80 percent of the meetings each year. If you have members who are highly committed and you really want to achieve intimacy within the group, six or seven total members also could be the right amount.

It is a good idea to start a small group, then slowly add members until you and the rest of the group believe you have the right number. You want to strive for a balance between having enough members to facilitate a large amount of experience and diverse viewpoints, while keeping the group small enough to achieve a high level of intimacy and trust. This will enable each of you to share real challenges and to give the opportunity for each of you to achieve real growth within the group over time.

If group members aren't really committed to prioritize their attendance, there won't be enough attendees at each meeting to give a full range of perspectives; the group won't be able to build the level of intimacy and trust required to have the maximum impact on each other and your businesses. So either do it right or don't do it. Take your time to search for high quality people who are willing to make a strong commitment, at least for two or three years, in order to make themselves and others better at running their businesses and their lives. There is no doubt that it will pay off.

I also would suggest that you politely contact anyone who is not adhering to the attendance expectations and ask about their overall level of commitment to the group. Most will probably either decide to start making attendance a priority or they quickly will admit to you that they simply have too many other priorities and need to step out of the group. One reason this is so important is that this person is taking away from the group because they are not there to give their input; they are taking another person's position who could be contributing to the group. The group needs to stay small, so when one person does not participate, they are denying the other members the benefits that could be gained from an additional person.

Another reason you need to be willing to politely confront a fellow business owner who is not active in group attendance or participation is that when this person attends sporadically, she or he can undermine the trust level of the whole group. Because they have not been there consistently to build trust with others, participants in the group will be less likely to share more intimate challenges and struggles they are having in their business. Also, the absentee member has not proven over time that he or she is committed enough to hear more confidential business items or challenges from others.

Don't allow people who are half-committed or sporadic in their commitment to undermine the integrity and the intimacy of the group. Just as you have to deal with problems within your business before they become a destructive presence that can cause your business to deteriorate, you must be willing to do the same with your peer support group. Otherwise, you won't fully reap the benefits of a cohesive, trusting, and supportive community of like-minded business owners.

The final fellow business-owner relationship that I recommend building is with a person who has a good bit more experience and success than you. This one person will become incredibly important to you and the success of your business. This person is your mentor. A mentor may work with you for a year, or she or he may work with you for a lifetime and become one of your very best friends.

Since your mentor is giving to you, let them determine how long they want to be in this role, as long as it is working. A mentor can be a relationship that simply develops naturally as you get to know another business owner in your community. More often than not though, due to everyone's busy schedules, you will need to seek a mentor, get to know them, then ask them if they would be willing to share some of their wisdom with you periodically over lunch or dinner.

If this person that you've identified and admire accepts your invitation, you may want to start by getting together for a meal once per quarter so that you can slowly build this relationship and see if it really works for both of you. A highly successful business owner is not going to have a lot of time to offer up to someone she or he barely knows, so be very respectful of their time and be careful not to ask for too much. Even if you only gain one or two meetings with them, they could be able to give you invaluable advice that you can refer back to for years to come.

Whenever you set a time to meet with this mentor, be sure to arrive a few minutes early, and try to limit their time with you to an hour or an hour and a half maximum. If this relationship really works and the mentor feels fulfilled by helping you grow, you both will know it and your time spent together may naturally become longer and more frequent. No matter how long you and your mentor walk this path together, never forget to show your appreciation and always leave the door open for them to discontinue this relationship at any time. If it is done right, they are giving you incredibly valuable information and accountability.

Since the mentor is not an employee of yours that is being compensated, you should look at every meeting as a gift. Your mentor may come to a point in which they believe they have taught you all they can and they may have another activity with which they would like to fill your time slot.

You also may come to a point in which you believe that your mentor has done all they can for you. Don't expect this to be a forever relationship and don't be afraid to end it or slow it down in frequency and time when appropriate. For instance, a once-per-year checkup may be the best course of action once your mentor has helped you achieve a certain level of growth.

I have two clients who are about 20 years apart in age and both are highly successful business owners in completely different industries. They have been meeting together regularly for lunch for over a decade. The older business owner has not only been an incredible mentor to the younger entrepreneur, but he has become a father figure to him and has taught him not only about business, but also has shaped his views on life and faith. I have had lunch with these two clients together and it is easy to tell that they love to be around each other. The younger business owner still shares his periodic challenges with this mentor and invites his advice. They have become the best of friends and have never grown tired of getting together on a regular basis. While this type of mentor relationship is highly unusual, it goes to show that you may receive a lot more than you could ever imagine by seeking guidance from another human being who has walked further down life's path than you have at the time. Have the courage to seek this type of relationship, and be willing to see what good things can potentially come out of it.

Another thought is that you may want to seek another mentor down the road who has a completely different approach to business, or who has a different skill set. Once you've mastered a particular approach to managing and growing your business, don't hesitate to be open to another viewpoint of a person who has had success through a different skill set and game plan. The more "tools in your tool belt," the better. Always be open to learning from others. My hope is that you always will find a joy and enthusiasm for learning new ways to help your business grow, to increase the profitability of your business, and to better serve your customers and your employees.

Since none of us have all of the answers, teaching each other what we do know is the best course of action to help all of us get better at what we do. This method also creates a lot of friendships and joy along the way.

I am a firm believer that if you stop learning, you stop leading. One of the things that keeps business owners enthusiastic and energized even into old age is that they never stop learning new things and growing in new ways. I am always amazed when I see highly successful business owners who are in their 80s, or sometimes even in their 90s, who still seem to have as much passion, or more passion, than business owners who are just starting out in their company.

One of my clients has built a highly successful Certified Public Accounting firm. This gentleman is well past the normal retirement age and has already turned over the reins to another C.P.A., as far as running the day-to-day operations of the practice. However, he is just as spry and enthusiastic about helping people with his professional skills as if he was in his 40s. He has never lost the joy of growing, learning, laughing, and building relationships with the people he works with in order to serve them with the skill set that God allowed him to develop over several decades. He has "been there and done that," so he has nothing left to prove.

The difference: This owner loves to mentor other younger C.P.A.s and still loves to utilize his rich level of experience to help businesses get off the ground. This older C.P.A. actually works with a lot of young entrepreneurs in order to help them make the best choices with their businesses early on and avoid potential pitfalls that could sabotage them. It is interesting to note that he seems to gain a youthful energy and enthusiasm from them, and they certainly gain wisdom and knowledge from his experience. So, they both come out better off than they ever would have been without each other.

If you're going to own and run your own business, get all of the good you can from it. Don't shortcut the advantages you can gain from mentoring others, partnering with peers, and being mentored yourself. After all, life is not just about having a hugely successful business and retiring wealthy, it is about the relationships you build and the lessons you learn along the way. It is a lot more fun and rewarding if you make it to the top with others whom you have grown to love and who have grown to love you.

People always say that it is lonely at the top. Well, that is not the case if you take others with you and if you have built relationships with those who have reached out their hand to pull you up.

Finally, remember that all of this mentoring is not just so you can build the most successful business in America; it is also implanted in you so that later you can pass this knowledge on to someone else. This can be a wonderful way for you to still reap the blessing of helping someone else beyond the life of your business. Mentoring another business owner is something you can do up into your 90s; it will help you maintain that child-like excitement that motivated you to start your own business in the first place.

You never get too old to give advice; there always will be others in life who could greatly benefit from hearing about the lessons you have learned. In addition to just growing your own business, you can have the joy and satisfaction of helping others to take their businesses to a whole new level. None of us were made to live in isolation. Make it a priority early in your business life to build camaraderie with others so that you are never "lonely at the top."

You also may find that in addition to simply mentoring someone, you may actually take enough interest in a younger, less experienced business owner to want to actually "sponsor" them. Sponsorship takes mentorship to a new level; you actually set out to open doors for this entrepreneur through making introductions and giving your recommendation on their behalf. While you obviously need to have a lot of trust and confidence in this business owner to attach part of your reputation to helping them grow their business, you may find over time that this is a tremendously rewarding experience for you both if you do connect with this type of person.

Be cautious going into this sponsoring role so that you are sure that the business owner you are trying to help is trustworthy. Be sure their business is truly at a level that it can back up any claims the business owner may make related to delivery of products or services. Someone made or will make openings for you, so embrace the ability to pass this to others who have earned it by building your trust over a sufficient period of time. This process involves giving to get. The more you give throughout the many cycles of your business career, the more you will get in return.

CHAPTER 9:

CHAPTER CHALLENGE

1. Do you already have a mentor or peer support group? If you do not have a mentor yet, this is a good time to start. This probably will not be a quick process. The younger you are in age (not in the development of your business), usually the easier it is to find a mentor.

   Many adults who are highly successful love to give back by mentoring a younger person. These individuals remember those who took time with them. They feel a sense of responsibility to pass this on, and to offer their advice and expertise to someone else who is just starting out or who is not as far down the path of success. Try to pursue this relationship with someone who really knows your industry, because the more similarities you two have, the more powerful their leadership and advice will be for you.

   If you are older and starting a business as a second or third career, plenty of hope is available for you as well. Don't feel that you are unusual to start up a business mid-life. There are a huge number of business owners who have chosen to take the expertise and contacts they have developed through other careers and put these to good use in starting their own business. The interesting thing is that you may find a mentor who is younger than you in age, but much farther along on the success scale in your particular industry. Don't be intimidated to take advantage of opportunities for mentorship with those who are younger or the same age as you, in this case. Experience and expertise are what you are looking for, not just gray hair.

2. Remember always to be respectful and courteous, as we discussed earlier in this chapter, and take the risk to ask for this type of relationship. All that person can say is "no," and if they do, this saves you time. You then can direct your efforts elsewhere to another person who may be a better fit.

Even if you have not started your business yet, a mentor may be just the ticket to help you get pre-pared to launch your business in the right way. However, don't waste the valuable time of a pro-fessional if you are not serious and if you don't already have many of your "ducks in a row." A fellow business owner does not have time to waste on a "dreamer" who has not already expended a respectable amount of effort getting their business ready to move forward. They also do not have time to waste on someone who is not willing to expend the effort to get the ball rolling and to keep it rolling forward. If you don't have the courage to move forward with your plan of launching or growing a business, don't use a mentor. It is wrong to use a mentor to simply allow yourself to fantasize about a business plan in order to escape the drudgery of your regular job and life in general (Remember, I told you that I would be "gut level" honest with you.).

3. Next, find a peer group that in some way compliments what you do or are planning to do in your business. Many trade organizations can put you into contact with other business owners in your chosen field or industry. Also, specialty organizations such as NAWBO (National Association of Women Business Owners), the Black Chamber of Commerce, the Hispanic Chamber of Commerce, and many others can support you in finding likeminded individuals who could be a sounding board and a professional and business resource for you.

    Give yourself 90 days as a time frame to find a mentor and a business support group. Don't be discouraged if it takes longer to find the right fit for a mentor. Just keep going. Once you get these initiatives under way, you will see how valuable they are and you will want to continue. If you have trouble finding the right fit, seek advice from your local Chamber of Commerce, or if all else fails, ask a commercial banker for recommendations and introductions.

CHAPTER 10:

HAVING FUN IS NOT WORK

Why would you go through all it takes to start your own business (the risk, the long hours, and the constant stress) if you don't have fun with it? For many, the American Dream is to own your own business. But you should only attempt this if you are passionate about supplying a need to others in a way that measures up to your own standards. It would be a shame to have this passion initially and go through the challenges of starting and running a business, without enjoying each phase of the process.

I certainly don't mean that a business owner should never feel down, discouraged, or frustrated. It comes with the territory of running a business, and of living life, for that matter. But you should maintain a continual and underlying joy in what you do. This not only makes you happier, but it tends to draw customers and employees to you, as well. Everyone tends to enjoy doing business with someone who is excited about what they do for a living. It also normally means that they are very good at what they do, because they enjoy it enough to spend a lot of time getting good at it and becoming an expert.

If owning your own business ever stops being fun, you would be better working for someone else. If you lose the joy long-term, you know it's time to make a change of some sort or possibly give it up altogether, and sell or shut down your business. Life is short. If you don't genuinely like and enjoy what you do for a living, find some other way to make a living. Be an asset, or be absent. There should be no "in-between." If you don't keep the enthusiasm for your business, you certainly can't expect those who work for you to keep it. Your less-than-great attitude can have too many negative consequences on too many employees and their families, so don't go there. If it ever stops being fun and challenging in an enjoyable way, put a step-by-step plan in place to move on to something else.

People who love their jobs, careers, and businesses have a light that shines in them that others can easily see. Some of this light comes from your overall attitude, and some of it comes from positioning yourself in a business that is a good fit for you. It allows you to use your natural, God-given strengths, expertise, and experiences. It is highly important to remind yourself each day that you don't have to go to work to build your business, but that you "get" to go to work to build your business. If you ever allow yourself to lose this attitude on a daily basis, it may be time to pack it up and head home. You always can go to work for someone else and not have the stress and pressure that owning and running a business brings.

Besides just enjoying the benefits of running your own business, there are other things you can do outside of your business to be sure that you remain fresh for the tasks at hand. Eating healthy, getting plenty of rest and regular exercise, and maintaining an active spiritual life are all important habits that will not only affect the health of your body, but also the health of your business. We also talked about the importance of building community with others in the last chapter. The healthier you are overall, the more energy and focus you will be able to put into your business and the more you will be able to contribute to its success. One thing you may not have thought about is how important a simple hobby can be to your long-term business success.

Of all the highly successful business owners that I've worked with over the past quarter of a century (who stayed in the same industry for 25 or more years), they all had one thing in common. That one thing was that they developed a hobby having nothing to do with their business. When you do stay in the same business in the same industry day after day, you achieve a level of excellence and greatness in that field that few obtain. However, you need something that takes you away from the business on a regular basis that provides a lot of fun and relaxation. Think about the successful people you know and what they do for fun. It may be mountain climbing, fly fishing, duck hunting, motorcycles, exotic cars, music, or any of an unlimited amount of options. A hobby is something you do or experience simply because you enjoy it without any concern about making money from it.

When you are "on" 24/7 like most business owners, even though you love what you do for a living, you have to have an escape. A hobby can be a healthy escape. If you don't plan regular healthy escapes, you may be tempted to find unhealthy ones such as drinking in excess, affairs, or being a workaholic. As my mom always said, "all work and no play makes Jack a dull boy." Too much work and not enough healthy escapes also make Jack, or Jill, burn out, and this is certainly not helpful to your productivity.

You may think that you have so much to do in your business that you don't have time to do whatever it is that you really enjoy doing. The truth is actually the opposite. Because you have so much to do and you want to be able to do it year after year, it is imperative that you take off at regular intervals to get away from your business and focus your mind on something completely different. This allows your brain to rest and your body to rejuvenate so that you are ready to go again at full speed when you get back to your business. In the long run, you will find yourself being much more productive, creative, and energetic if you get away from the office at regular intervals for some play time.

Because a business owner's schedule seems to always be full, take time right now and block off one week per quarter for the next year for the sole purpose of having fun and getting away. If you are too early in the formation of your business to do this, at least block off two days per quarter to get away on a Thursday and Friday so that you can have a long weekend to look forward to and to benefit from.

One of the big advantages of making plans to enjoy fun hobbies and trips well in advance is that it gives you a lot of time to look forward to these getaway adventures. This buildup of excitement that happens prior to your time away can be just the thing to get you through those trying challenges at your company and the long hours that you sometimes, or often, work. You are able to see that in the not too distant future a fun "payoff" is coming for all of the hard work you are doing. Hobbies and time off are a tangible reward for the effort you expend and the price you pay to own and run your own business.

One of my clients put in long hours over the years to build a highly successful veterinary practice. His hobby or "escape" became fun family vacations. While this veterinarian loved running his practice and taking care of people's prized pets with health problems, he kept fresh for his business through a traveling hobby. Somehow his practice "survived" those weeks each year without him and it allowed other veterinarians working in the practice to gain more experience and leadership practice.

Granted, a lot of vacation hours may not be realistic for you at this time if you are just starting your business, or if you are still early on in the development of your business. However, you can and you must do something to get away for some time on a consistent basis, no matter how inexpensive or brief of a "get away" it may be. The point is to develop a "hobby habit" early on in your life as a business owner so that this simple and fun exercise can give you the breathing room you need to regenerate and keep going.

When you think about it, one of the main motivators for people who own their own business is to be able to be their own boss and to reap solid financial rewards. If you are so tied to your business that you can't take a day off to enjoy life and to spend some of that extra money you are making, then how is a business giving you the freedoms that you started it for in the first place? Being your own boss is only attractive if you are the kind of boss with yourself who appreciates your hard work enough to insist that you take some time off periodically to enjoy the fruits of your labor. If you become a task master with yourself in your business, then you would be better off having a boss other than yourself who would treat you in a kinder manner.

Think about it. Are you a good boss to yourself? Do you reward yourself with spending a reasonable amount on hobbies that you enjoy? Do you encourage and require yourself to step off the treadmill of your business on a consistent basis so that you can relax and recharge your batteries? Being your own boss is great if you treat yourself like you should be treated. Unfortunately, a lot of business owners don't realize how poorly they treat themselves and they go through life wearing themselves out to make money that they don't even have time to spend.

I learned of a successful entrepreneur who had grown his business to a highly profitable, national company and had reaped financial rewards beyond what many of us dream about. This business owner was active in his church; the area of ministry that he volunteered for each week (and had done so for years) was in helping church attendees obtain parking before the service started. That's right, he was one of the guys in the parking lot wearing orange vests and directing cars. Quite surprising for the owner and CEO of a huge national company, right? You would have thought that he would have been chairman of the finance committee or chairman of the personnel committee for this large church, due to his excellent leadership and decision-making capabilities.

This man was tasked each week with leading his business successfully, yet he still wanted to honor his God by giving of his time and service. He found an area of ministry that he could do that gave him the ability to rejuvenate himself on a weekly basis. He told people in the church that he absolutely loved having virtually no responsibility other than to serve in the simple task of helping worshippers to find a good, close parking place to the sanctuary. On Sundays there was no pressure to perform, no demand on his time, and no drain on his intelligence, because he was able to transform himself into a parking-lot attendant.

This business owner was given the ability not to take himself too seriously and to stay in touch with just being a regular guy. He could talk to congregation members in the parking lot, many of whom had no idea about who he was, without the misconceptions that often accompany someone who is highly successful and wealthy. Not only was this good for him personally, it also helped him to be able to relate to everyone who worked at his company, even to the lowest level employee.

Be proactive early on to find hobbies and ministry opportunities that are different from what you do to earn a living and to run a company, and be sure to create the time for them. Instead of detracting from your business, you will end up breathing more life into yourself and your business. In addition, it will give you more areas in which you can relate to others. The more diversified you are, the more commonalities you can find with your employees and your customers. It also makes life a lot more enjoyable.

Along with keeping passion in your work and developing an enjoyable hobby, my final piece of advice is to strive for a balanced life. Though being a business owner often demands a lot of hours at the company, you must have boundaries that still allow time for faith, family, friends, and fun. While being a successful and prosperous business owner is a huge asset, that alone will not fulfill you. I have worked with quite a few business owners who allowed their businesses to become their lives. Success and money are not that great if you have no one you love to share it with, or if you have ruined your health in exchange for these benefits.

The grounding you obtain from a balanced life will give you strength to withstand the storms that come your way as a business owner. Strive to keep the "6 Fs" in good balance within your life as a business owner: faith, family, finances, friends, fitness, and fun. Your business should provide time and resources for each of these categories and each of these categories will also turn around and provide strength for running your business as well.

CHAPTER 10:

CHAPTER CHALLENGE

1. Well, you have completed all of the previous challenges, I trust. This one is the most exciting and the most enjoyable. It is the main reason you go through all of the previous exercises to launch and build a successful business. Now it's time to have fun!

   Do you have a favorite hobby that is not related to your business or the field of your business? If so, how much time do you set aside to spend on this hobby each month? I recommend that you do at least one thing for a minimum of an hour each week that is related to your favorite hobby. This could be as simple as reading several pages out of a book each week or watching a documentary about your hobby. You need to keep the "feel good" juices flowing that come from the enjoyment you get from a particular hobby or passion. Again, this is not about making it into a commercial enterprise. This is about simply having fun and getting enjoyment from something you like to do, with no pressure of having to make money at it. If you don't really have a hobby, you need to think about the things you have enjoyed in life and pick one pursuit that can bring a smile to your face and relaxation to your body.

I always had a passion for performing and writing music, but I learned I was not talented enough to make a career out of it. Now I love to listen to all types of music, go to concerts, watch documentaries on famous musicians and bands, and watch music performances of all types at a local university near me. I actually have served on a Friends of the Arts Board at Belmont University in Nashville, where I was invited to a lot of student performances, allowed to meet and hear from visiting artists and directors, and get to know and encourage a lot of music students who are working hard to take their God-given musical talents to a professional level. It has nothing to do with banking, and I like it that way. I love what I do for a living, but I also get refreshed for my banking career by being around music on a regular basis.

2. Besides setting up yourself with a fun hobby that can bring a lifetime of joy, be sure that you are building a balanced life. Business owners who don't start off with a balanced approach often can work themselves into an addiction in which their business consumes all of their time, energy, and devotion. This is a recipe for disaster, both personally and professionally.

    You need to have a spiritual life, a family life, disciplined financial choices, hobbies and fun time, relaxation and rest, exercise, and a healthy eating and overall healthy lifestyle regimen to truly thrive over the long-term. All of these areas will give you stability and strength to enable you to be stronger for building and running your business.

3. Take time to rate yourself on a "1 to 10" score in all of these areas: spiritual, family, finances, friends, hobbies, rest, exercise, and healthy eating and lifestyle. Anything at a 6 or below certainly needs some work. You want to build yourself and your business for the long haul; a balanced life can give you the strength to do this.

    Don't take the easy way out and become another workaholic business owner or a business owner who simply lives to make more and more of the "almighty" dollar. Exercise the discipline that it takes to build a well-balanced life and you will be richer in every way for it. If needed, spend one day per month over six months meeting with a friend, or engage a life coach once per month who can help you make changes and hold you accountable so that these changes can be sustained. Build yourself right and you will have the tools to build your business right as well.

CONCLUSION

I f there's one thing in this book to remind you about, it would be that you need to be sure that you are really excited and passionate about the business you want to start before you begin this grand adventure. Or, if you are down the road with your business and you are not truly enjoying the life you have created, it is definitely time to reevaluate your situation. Life is too short, and a business owner's hours are too long when you are not in your area of passion. You are taking on entirely too much responsibility, risk, and pressure not to enjoy it.

Remember, it is easy to follow someone who loves what they do, and it is easy to sell something when you truly believe in it. If you are going to be the lead person who starts and builds the business, you need to be sure that you are in the right area of your expertise and passion so you can do what you do naturally and from a position of maximum strength.

Once you get well positioned in the right industry and the best fitting line of work for you, don't shortcut the process. It takes a lot of time for an acorn to become a towering oak tree. In the same way, it takes a lot of work and learning on the front end to build a successful business. The deeper your roots, the taller your tree can grow. If you try to jumpstart the process without taking time to learn the ropes and build the proper amount of experience on the front end, you will pay for it one way or the other on the back end.

Every boxer has warm-up fights before they take on the champion. In the same way, you are wise if you allow yourself to learn your trade working for someone else while all of the responsibility and financial investment is not on you. Paying your dues by getting years of experience prior to launching your own company can give you a great head start while saving you lots of costly mistakes when it hurts the most. Most mature businesses have enough guardrails in place to keep an employee from hurting the company in a major way. However, when it is your own business and you make a bad call or an unwise decision, it can cost you dearly in money, reputation, and recovery time. You need to put yourself in a position to make the big mistakes early when you are working for someone else, so the mistakes in your own business are smaller and less costly. Your patience and persistence will be rewarded down the road.

As you accept the adventure of starting your own business, challenges definitely will occur along the way, and there may be times when you will want to give up or go a different direction. Resist this urge if you ever want to accomplish what you set out to do in the first place. For a long period of time you will have to maintain your focus in the same direction you started if you really desire to reap a large reward. Success will not come easy for you, just as it hasn't come easy for anyone else who has traveled down this path of business ownership.

When the challenges seem the greatest and your payoff seems the farthest away is the time when it is absolutely necessary that you hang on like there is no tomorrow. In the long-term, if you truly want to gain the rewards of running a successful business, you have to stay the course in the face of discouragement and hopelessness. In September 2001 one of my clients had ventured to build a new facility and expand his product offerings (and debt) when 9/11 hit. He had made a calculated decision to grow his business to the next level while never having a clue that an outside force was coming against his business that had nothing to do with him or his decision making. I remember talking to him right after 9/11 happened. He said that it might be tough, but that he had made this decision and he was going to somehow see it through.

See it through is exactly what he did. He did what he had to do each day to keep his business running. He stayed in the fight for the success of his business and never gave up. When the economy came back and demand for his business increased, he used the new building and product offerings to take advantage of an opportunity to increase his sales. Years later, this business owner sold his business for a huge profit; he retired with a satisfying financial situation that will serve him well until he dies.

How did he do it? He didn't give up or give in when conventional wisdom told him that he was in a battle that could capsize his ship. What would have happened if he had given up and thrown in the towel? He would probably be working for someone else without a solid plan for retirement. You have to maintain your commitment to stay in the fight when other, less courageous people, would give up and bail out. You have to "stay in line" and vow to see your business through to success on the other side. You must believe that failure is not an option, and therefore, quitting isn't either.

Also, be as committed to growing slowly as you are to staying in the fight. Baby steps are the key so that you can remain in a position of strength in order to hang on through the tough times. Those who want to get rich quick usually end up in poverty because they do not have the inner strength and discipline to systematically build something in a calculated way. In the same way, those who try to grow a business at a very rapid pace usually see it unwind before their eyes.

Growing little by little allows you to stretch yourself and your business in reasonable amounts that do not tax your business with too much strain. Just like a weightlifter who desires to grow in strength cannot add 50 pounds at a time without damaging muscles due to the strain, a business owner cannot add too much too fast, or she or he will damage the business and themselves by the strain of the extra load.

Be careful with keeping your ego in check as you see success in your business, as this can often throw you off a solid, sustainable path of growth. When you suddenly think you are too successful to fail, there is a temptation to grow more in quick fashion because you think you can do no wrong. This is often a point when a business owner becomes vulnerable to his or her ego—a dangerous place to be. It takes a lot more internal strength to discipline yourself to wait for rewards and to consistently grow over time than it does to "put the pedal to the metal" just because things have been going well and you want to get rewarded more rapidly for the efforts you have put in so far.

Ego also can derail your decision making if you desire for your business to be at the same level as others. True strength is not how fast you can grow or how quickly you can get to the top of the mountain. It is in how disciplined you are over time to do the daily things that over the weeks, months, years, and even decades steadily increase the growth and profitability of your business. This is how you build a business that will last and be consistently profitable year after year. You do it little by little and keep your eyes on your own business progress instead of trying to keep up with everyone else. It takes a lot of discipline and is not the easy way; slow and steady growth is what you want, and this will keep your business strong through the years.

In addition, even if your personality is not one that enjoys socializing on a regular basis, don't neglect the joy and the benefit of networking with others in your community. It gives you an ability to be able to speak for and against things in your community and city, builds your credibility, and helps promote the goodwill of your business. People are much more likely to do business with someone who takes a personal interest in the community and who volunteers on a regular basis to help others in their time of need. Being out and about, meeting new people while working to help others, then getting to share about your company in casual settings can reap huge benefits for you and your business over time.

One of my friends is an insurance agent, and he has worked tirelessly with various causes around the community where I live near Nashville. He always has a bright smile on his face and usually is doing or saying something to make others laugh or smile. This man also has grown his insurance agency by leaps and bounds through the contacts he has made with fellow citizens who appreciate his welcoming smile and his support of their community. He has made lots of friends and gained many customers by getting out of his office, networking in the community, and working together for the common good of all in his city.

Chapter 6 talks about storing cash. This should be done before you go into business and every chance you get once you are in business. There will always be challenging times that come along unexpectedly in your business and in the economy. While you rarely see them coming, they will indeed come. When the economy turns south, cash is king because it is the only thing other than profit that can pay your bills and keep your business afloat. Many business owners and investors like to have as little cash as possible because they want every dollar they have to be working for them to make more dollars. This is a good concept until the cash flow temporarily dries up or takes a downturn. At that point, you can lose a lot of those dollars you have previously made because you are in a financial straight jacket due to having very little or no liquidity.

A good example is during the unexpected pandemic of 2020. When the economy was temporarily shut down in the second quarter of the year due to COVID-19, many businesses couldn't last even two or three weeks because they had no reserves. They were living on the cash flow that came every week, and every dollar that came in was going for expenses and salaries. So, when revenue temporarily stopped, it became a crisis overnight for many business owners.

On the other hand, some business owners had saved for a rainy day and were able to move forward until better times came because they had prepared when the economy was booming. Joseph was a man in the Bible who had a vision from God that seven years of famine were coming to Egypt after seven years of plenty. Joseph was wise enough to encourage the Pharaoh of Egypt to allow him to store away tons of grain during the seven years of plenty so they could successfully make it through the next seven years of famine.

Most of us will not be fortunate enough to receive a vision from God of exactly when hard times will hit. But we won't have to if we simply will adhere to the principle of storing cash in the good times. Then we always will be prepared for an economic or industry downturn. This liquidity will give us choices and time to maneuver when otherwise we would be constricted and left without good options.

Another word of wisdom: The one who hires the best team wins. It is often that simple. There is a lot to be said for how you coach and lead that team, but the talent on the team determines a lot of the potential that your company will have for greatness. Therefore, go after the best and don't stop until they are playing on your team.

Also, top talent likes to work with other top talent, so your best recruiting tool will be the people you initially hire in your business. You will likely duplicate the level of talent you initially acquire, so getting the best people possible on the front end will make a huge difference in the quality of your entire team.

Start recruiting now and don't stop until you sell your business or turn it over to someone else. Recruiting is a job that you will always have as a business owner and it is a skill that you will want to continue to improve upon. It is very likely one of the best things you can do for the health and success of your business.

Additionally, solid recruiting is the best way to ensure that you don't have to work all the time to keep your business thriving. If you hire great people and give them freedom to create, while also giving them credit for what they contribute, your business can thrive even while you take some time off and enjoy the fruits of your labor. It is humbling—but necessary—to see that your business becomes great because of the people on your team, and not just because of *you*. The quicker you see and embrace this concept, the better your business and the better your life will be.

Chapter 8 encourages you not to run away *from* accountability, but to run *toward* it. You being the boss and the one who started and who owns the business does not mean that you are not still accountable. You are accountable to your employees, to your customers, and if you are smart, to other professionals. These professionals can utilize their expertise to assist you in keeping your business between the guardrails as you continue to drive your business toward more growth.

Remember, to *have* authority, you have to *be under* authority. Your decisions and forward progress are so much more potent if you allow your C.P.A., attorney, banker, and investment advisor to give their professional input before you make decisions that will affect the financial future of your business and your personal financial life, as well. No one knows everything and no one is above making mistakes.

Wise is the woman or man who has enough humility to ask for and accept the advice of others who are in their circle of trust. You still make the final call, but at least you do so after having received the counsel of those who are in place to protect you and assist you in reaping the highest financial rewards possible. Once a decision is made and you move forward, it is often too late to go back.

Always obtain advisement on the front end, consider all the options and potential consequences, then make a reasonable decision after having received the advice and counsel from your intimate group of financial and legal experts. This practice will help you to avoid at least 80 percent of the obstacles that can sabotage your business and your personal financial well-being.

Also, in your quest for accountability and guidance, don't neglect the benefits and blessings to be gained from having a support group of fellow business owners. These comrades not only will give you valuable insight as you walk through the years of growing and managing your business, but they ultimately will become some of your best friends and strongest supporters. You will gain as much from them as they gain from you; you all will be better because of the interaction that you have together.

Everyone has a different perspective and often a different strength to share. Therefore, it is wise to take advantage of the insight and guidance you can receive from other business owners who are learning and growing right along with you.

Choosing a mentor who can guide you through the many challenges you will face in running a business will help you to take advantage of many gains while also avoiding many pitfalls. If you want to be wise, hang out with the wise, listen to the wise, and do what the wise do. Mentors will share their wisdom with you, then you, in turn, will be able to pass this wisdom along to someone else. Your life will be richer, your wallet or purse fuller, and your joy more complete when you walk this path with others. Getting to the top together is much more satisfying than trying to do it by yourself.

Finally, have fun! Don't ever sacrifice enjoying your life for anything, including the pressures that sometimes come with owning and running a business. Never forget that you started down this road because you wanted to live your dream, have a better-than-normal life, and do something different and exciting. Keep your enthusiasm, excitement, and drive. Don't let the challenges and problems that come your way push you off the track you started out on when you began your business in the first place. You have paid the price to do your own thing and live life on your own schedule;

don't allow anything to get in your way of living the fun and adventurous life you chose.

If you don't laugh some each day and smile a lot, ask yourself why. As a business owner, you have been given a unique gift to have more direct control over your life, schedule, and finances. Take advantage of this special opportunity and make the most of it. Never forget how blessed you are and how good God has been to you.

You are in a great position to help others, including your employees, customers, fellow business owners, and community. Do all the good you can to all of people you can in all the ways you can all the time you can. Use your influence as the owner of your own business to help others and to make this world a better place. Remember, power is given to you to help others and not to puff up yourself. Go forward and do good and use your influence in the right way.

At the end of your journey, you will have done more than just have a successful business and (hopefully) a lot of money, you will have made life better for a whole lot of people, and will have built some amazing friendships and memories along the way.

Finally, take some of that hard-earned money you make and take fun trips, pamper yourself and your family, and experience a lot of fun adventures. Don't give in to simply being a workaholic who is always "on" and never can get away from the business. This is never the correct mindset. You work hard so you can play hard, so you can do fun and exciting things, and so you can live life to the fullest. In life we always reap what we sow. So, work hard, but step away from work and play like a child. Not only will you end up enjoying life much more, but you actually will find that you become more successful in your business as your life builds and maintains this kind of balance.

I hope that you have found at least one or two "jewels" from our time together that you can immediately begin to put into practice with your new or existing business. It is my wish that you achieve tremendous success in your business, not only in financial terms, but in the positive ways that you impact the lives of your employees, customers, family, and community.

ABOUT THE AUTHOR

John Bennett grew up in the small town of Ila, Georgia, and moved to Nashville, Tennessee in 1986 to attend Belmont University. After graduating with a degree in Finance from Belmont, he spent a period of time in the music business before moving into the financial services field in 1996. He began a banking career in which he started at an entry level position and worked his way into being the Market President for three different banks in Nashville. John is also a graduate of the Tennessee Bankers Association School of Banking and a graduate of the Tennessee Bankers Association School of Commercial Lending. In addition, he has completed post-graduate coursework in various classes in the areas of finance and banking. John's passion is working with business owners to help them achieve the maximum growth and success possible in their business. During his 25-year career in banking, he has worked with hundreds of successful business owners in almost every industry imaginable.

John's goal for this book is to share the wisdom he has learned from his banking career through working with successful businesses. His writing appeals to entrepreneurs across the spectrum, from beginners who dream of starting their own business, to those who already run a successful business and simply want to constantly improve at growing and leading the business they began many years ago. John is a Christian who sees it as his personal calling to help those who lead businesses to be as successful and as intentional as possible with the influence that they have been given, in order to make life better for their employees, customers, families, and communities.

John lives in Nashville, Tennessee, with his wife Paula. The Bennetts have four grown children: Anna, Edward, Jonathan, and Angelia. John enjoys writing and speaking to audiences about various business topics. He also loves to write and listen to all types of music and watch old TV shows and westerns.

John Bennett can be contacted for speaking engagements and training services at builditrightjohnbennett@gmail.com.

CPSIA information can be obtained
at www.ICGtesting.com
Printed in the USA
LVHW011914220821
695822LV00008B/210